React: Build Dynamic User Interfaces for Web and Mobile Apps

A Comprehensive Guide to Mastering React for Full-Stack Development

BOOZMAN RICHARD

BOOKER BLUNT

Table of Content

TABLE OF CONTENTS

4

INTRODUCTION

Mastering React: Building Dynamic Web and Mobile Apps

Welcome to **"Mastering React: Building Dynamic Web and Mobile Apps"**, a comprehensive guide designed to take you on a journey from the foundational concepts of React to building full-fledged applications for both the web and mobile platforms. Whether you're a beginner starting your React journey or an experienced developer looking to deepen your understanding, this book offers a structured and engaging approach to mastering React.

React is undoubtedly one of the most popular and powerful libraries for building user interfaces. With its component-based architecture, declarative programming model, and large ecosystem, React has revolutionized the way developers create dynamic and interactive UIs. What began as a library for building simple web interfaces has now evolved into a versatile tool for building both web and mobile apps, thanks to **React Native**. The flexibility and performance of React allow developers to create seamless experiences, from simple static websites to highly complex, full-featured applications.

In this book, we will dive deep into the core features of React and its ecosystem, breaking down complex topics into clear, digestible chapters. You'll gain a solid understanding of React concepts, best practices, and advanced techniques that will allow you to build scalable, high-performance applications. This book covers a wide range of topics to ensure you're well-equipped to tackle real-world development challenges.

What You Will Learn

This book is organized to provide you with a strong foundation in React while also preparing you for more advanced topics and mobile development with React Native. Here's a look at what you'll explore throughout this book:

1. **Introduction to React and the Basics**:
   - You'll begin by understanding the core concepts of React, including the component model, JSX, and state management. You'll learn how to build basic components, manage state, and handle user interactions.
2. **Advanced React Concepts**:
   - As you progress, we will dive into more advanced topics, such as the Context API, component lifecycle methods, hooks (like useState, useEffect, and custom hooks), and optimizing React performance. You'll also learn how to

handle asynchronous data fetching, manage side effects, and implement error boundaries.

3. **State Management in React**:
   o Managing state efficiently in React is key to building scalable apps. You'll learn about different state management techniques, including local component state, the Context API, and Redux for global state management. We'll explore how Redux helps in large-scale applications and how you can implement it for more robust app architecture.

4. **Building Web and Mobile Apps**:
   o With React, you'll be able to create powerful web apps, and with **React Native**, you'll be able to extend your React knowledge to build mobile apps for both iOS and Android. We'll cover the differences between React for the web and React Native, giving you the skills to handle both platforms effectively.

5. **Handling Routing, Forms, and Data**:
   o Learn how to manage navigation between pages with React Router, and how to build dynamic forms with validation and error handling. We'll also cover how to fetch data from APIs and display it efficiently, creating apps that are both interactive and performant.

6. **Progressive Web Apps (PWAs)**:
   o You'll discover how to make your React apps work offline, improve performance, and offer an app-like experience using **Progressive Web Apps (PWAs)**. We'll walk you through the steps of converting your React app into a fully functional PWA.

7. **Deployment and Best Practices**:
   o We will wrap up by discussing the deployment of React apps to popular platforms like **Netlify**, **Vercel**, and **Heroku**. You'll learn how to configure your app for production, optimize it for performance, and deploy it to a live server.

8. **Advanced Topics and Continuous Learning**:
   o React is constantly evolving, and in the final chapters, we'll explore the latest trends and features, such as **React Concurrent Mode**, **React Server Components**, and more. We'll also cover how to keep learning as a React developer, the best practices for building full-stack applications, and resources to keep your skills sharp and up to date.

Who This Book is For

This book is designed for developers of all levels, whether you're just starting with React or looking to level up your skills. The chapters begin with beginner-friendly content, gradually progressing to advanced topics that cater to professional developers looking to master React and build production-ready applications.

If you are:

- A **beginner** who wants to learn how to build React apps from the ground up.
- An **intermediate developer** looking to explore more advanced React patterns, state management with Redux, and mobile development with React Native.
- An **experienced developer** seeking to stay up-to-date with the latest React trends and tools, and dive into building both web and mobile apps.

This book will guide you through practical, hands-on examples, making it easier to understand the theory and apply it in real-world scenarios.

Why Learn React?

React has quickly become the go-to library for modern web and mobile development, and for good reason. Its **component-based architecture**, **declarative UI model**, and **one-way data flow** make it easy to manage complex applications while maintaining high performance. Additionally, with the power of **React Native**, developers can now use their React skills to build **native mobile apps** for both iOS and Android using the same codebase.

Learning React will not only make you a better web and mobile developer but will also allow you to take full advantage of the rapidly-growing ecosystem surrounding React. React's vast community, libraries, and tools make it one of the most powerful frameworks for building dynamic user interfaces.

How This Book Will Help You Master React

- **Practical Approach**: We focus on providing hands-on, real-world examples to reinforce each concept. Each chapter is filled with practical exercises and examples that you can implement in your own projects right away.
- **Clear Explanations**: Complex topics are broken down into easy-to-understand sections, making it simple to follow and learn at your own pace.
- **Comprehensive Coverage**: This book covers everything you need to know about React, from the basics to advanced techniques and even mobile development with React Native. By the end of this book, you'll be equipped with the skills to build sophisticated web and mobile applications.
- **Future-Proofing**: React is a continuously evolving library, and we've ensured that the content includes the

latest features and updates, so you're always working with the best tools available.

Conclusion

"Mastering React: Building Dynamic Web and Mobile Apps" is more than just a guide to learning React; it's a comprehensive roadmap to becoming a **full-stack React developer** capable of building high-quality, scalable applications for the web and mobile platforms. Whether you're building a simple to-do list app or a complex enterprise-level system, the tools and techniques covered in this book will empower you to create robust, performant apps.

Let's dive into the world of React and build powerful, dynamic applications together. Happy coding!

CHAPTER 1

INTRODUCTION TO REACT

Overview of React and Its Role in Modern Web and Mobile Development

React is a JavaScript library developed by Facebook (now Meta) that allows developers to build dynamic user interfaces (UIs) for web and mobile applications. It has gained widespread popularity due to its component-based architecture, which makes development more efficient, scalable, and maintainable.

React's main strength lies in its ability to build interactive UIs by managing state and rendering components efficiently. Unlike traditional approaches where the UI was directly manipulated by updating the DOM (Document Object Model), React uses a virtual DOM, an in-memory representation of the real DOM. This allows React to minimize direct manipulation of the DOM, resulting in faster rendering and a more responsive user interface.

React's versatility extends beyond the web. With **React Native**, developers can leverage their React knowledge to build mobile apps for iOS and Android. This unified framework allows web and mobile applications to share logic, components, and even design patterns.

In the context of full-stack development, React acts as the front-end interface that communicates with back-end services, APIs, and databases, providing users with dynamic and real-time data updates.

Why React is Popular for Building Dynamic User Interfaces

React has revolutionized the way developers approach front-end development, especially in creating complex, dynamic user interfaces. Here's why it has become so popular:

1. **Component-Based Architecture**: React applications are built using components, which are self-contained, reusable pieces of code that manage their own state. This leads to better maintainability, as developers can work on individual components without worrying about the entire UI.

2. **Declarative Syntax**: React allows developers to describe the UI in a declarative way, meaning you only need to specify what the UI should look like for a given state, and React takes care of the rest. This simplifies development and makes the code more readable.

3. **Virtual DOM**: React's virtual DOM ensures minimal updates to the real DOM by determining what parts of the UI need to be updated. This results in improved

performance, as React only updates the necessary elements.

4. **Unidirectional Data Flow**: React enforces a one-way data flow, making it easier to manage and debug the application state. Data is passed down from parent to child components via props, and state changes are handled in the components themselves.

5. **Rich Ecosystem**: React boasts a large ecosystem of tools and libraries that simplify development. From React Router for navigation to Redux for state management, React developers have access to a variety of resources to handle complex use cases.

6. **Cross-Platform Development with React Native**: With React Native, developers can write mobile applications for iOS and Android using the same knowledge of React. This allows for cross-platform development with shared codebases and a faster time-to-market.

7. **Active Community and Corporate Backing**: Being developed by Facebook and maintained by an active community of developers, React benefits from constant updates, improvements, and a vast amount of resources, tutorials, and support.

Setting Up the React Development Environment

To get started with React, you need to set up a development environment. Here's a simple guide to help you set up React for your first project:

1. **Install Node.js**: React requires Node.js to run. Node.js is a runtime environment for JavaScript that allows you to run JavaScript on the server side. To install Node.js, visit nodejs.org and download the latest LTS (Long Term Support) version.

2. **Install npm (Node Package Manager)**: npm is bundled with Node.js and helps you manage libraries and packages in your project. Once you have Node.js installed, npm should already be available in your system.

3. **Create a React Application**: The easiest way to set up a React app is by using **Create React App**, a tool that sets up the basic structure of your project for you.

   o Open your terminal (or Command Prompt) and run the following command to install Create React App globally:

   bash

   ```
   npm install -g create-react-app
   ```

   o Now, create a new React project by running:

```
bash
```

```
npx create-react-app my-first-react-
app
```

- o This will create a new folder called `my-first-react-app` with all the necessary files and dependencies.

4. **Navigate to Your Project Folder**: Go into your project directory to start the development server:

```
bash
```

```
cd my-first-react-app
```

5. **Start the Development Server**: Run the following command to start the React development server:

```
bash
```

```
npm start
```

- o This will launch your app in the browser, and you can start working on your React project.

A Simple "Hello World" Example to Get Started

Now that you have your development environment set up, let's create a simple "Hello World" React app.

1. **Open src/App.js**: This is where the main content of your app is located. The default code in App.js looks something like this:

   javascript

   ```javascript
   import React from 'react';
   import './App.css';

   function App() {
     return (
       <div className="App">
         <h1>Hello, React!</h1>
       </div>
     );
   }

   export default App;
   ```

2. **Modify the Code**: Replace the `<h1>Hello, React!</h1>` with a personalized message, for example:

   javascript

```
import React from 'react';
import './App.css';

function App() {
  return (
    <div className="App">
      <h1>Hello,    World!    Welcome    to
React.</h1>
    </div>
  );
}

export default App;
```

3. **Save and View the Changes**: After saving the file, your development server (running from `npm start`) should automatically reload the page, and you will see the message "Hello, World! Welcome to React." displayed on your webpage.

Conclusion

This chapter provided an introduction to React, explaining its role in modern web and mobile development, why it's popular for building dynamic UIs, and how to set up the development environment. You also got your hands dirty with a simple "Hello World" example to kickstart your React journey. In the next chapter, we will dive deeper into the core concepts of React, such as components, JSX, and state, laying the foundation for more advanced topics later in the book.

CHAPTER 2

UNDERSTANDING THE BASICS OF REACT

Introduction to Components: Functional and Class-Based

In React, **components** are the building blocks of a user interface. They allow developers to break down a complex UI into smaller, reusable pieces. React components come in two main forms: **functional components** and **class-based components**. Both types can manage state and handle events, but they differ in their syntax and lifecycle management.

1. **Functional Components**: Functional components are simpler and easier to understand. They are JavaScript functions that return a JSX element. With the introduction of **React Hooks** in version 16.8, functional components gained the ability to manage state and perform side effects, which was previously only possible with class-based components.

   Here's an example of a functional component:

   ```
   javascript
   ```

```
function Greeting() {
    return    <h1>Hello,    welcome    to
React!</h1>;
}
```

- o In this example, the `Greeting` component is a function that returns JSX.
- o Functional components are the preferred choice for most new React code because of their simplicity and the power of hooks.

2. **Class-Based Components**: Before React Hooks, class-based components were the main way to define components that manage state or lifecycle methods. Class-based components are more verbose but still used in legacy codebases.

Here's an example of a class-based component:

javascript

```
class Greeting extends React.Component {
    render() {
        return    <h1>Hello,    welcome    to
React!</h1>;
    }
}
```

- o The `Greeting` component is defined as a class that extends `React.Component`.
- o The `render()` method returns JSX, which tells React how to render the component.

While class-based components are still widely used in existing projects, **functional components** with hooks are the future of React development, offering a cleaner, more concise approach to building components.

JSX: What It Is and Why It Matters

JSX, or **JavaScript XML**, is a syntax extension for JavaScript that allows you to write HTML-like code inside JavaScript. It is a key feature of React, enabling developers to describe the UI structure in a declarative way.

1. **What is JSX?** JSX is not a new language; it is a combination of JavaScript and HTML that makes writing React components more intuitive. React uses JSX to create elements that are rendered in the virtual DOM.

   Here's an example of JSX:

   ```javascript
   const element = <h1>Hello, world!</h1>;
   ```

- o In this example, the JSX code is very similar to HTML. However, JSX has some key differences, such as using `className` instead of `class` for CSS classes, as `class` is a reserved keyword in JavaScript.

2. **Why JSX Matters?** JSX is important for a few reasons:
   - o **Readability**: It allows developers to write UI components in a familiar syntax, making the code more readable and maintainable.
   - o **Declarative Syntax**: With JSX, you describe the UI at a given point in time, and React takes care of updating the UI when the underlying data changes.
   - o **Integration with JavaScript**: Since JSX is just JavaScript, you can embed expressions and logic directly into your components, making your code dynamic.

3. **Behind the Scenes of JSX**: JSX is not directly understood by browsers. Instead, React compiles it into regular JavaScript. When you write JSX, tools like Babel (a JavaScript compiler) convert it into `React.createElement()` calls, which are used to create the virtual DOM elements.

For example, the JSX:

```javascript
```

24

```
<h1>Hello, world!</h1>
```

Compiles to:

```
javascript
```

```
React.createElement('h1',   null,   'Hello,
world!');
```

React then compares the virtual DOM with the real DOM and updates it as necessary.

Rendering UI with React Components

In React, the process of **rendering** refers to taking your components and displaying them in the browser. This happens in a two-step process:

1. **React Elements**: React elements are the smallest building blocks of a React app. They describe what should appear on the screen and are the result of rendering JSX in components.
2. **ReactDOM**: ReactDOM is responsible for rendering these elements to the actual DOM in the browser.

The typical flow of rendering in React is as follows:

- You define components that return JSX (React elements).
- React takes these elements, creates a virtual DOM, and then efficiently updates the real DOM to match the virtual one.

To render a React component, you use the `ReactDOM.render()` method. This is how React "mounts" the component to the actual DOM.

Here's a simple example of rendering a component:

```javascript
import React from 'react';
import ReactDOM from 'react-dom';

function App() {
  return <h1>Hello, world!</h1>;
}

// Rendering the App component inside the root div element
ReactDOM.render(<App />,
document.getElementById('root'));
```

- In this example, the `App` component returns a simple JSX element (`<h1>Hello, world!</h1>`).
- `ReactDOM.render()` takes the `App` component and renders it inside the HTML element with the id of `root`.

26

The rendered output will be an <h1> element on the webpage, displaying "Hello, world!".

Hands-on Example: Creating a Simple Static Web Page with React

Let's walk through creating a simple static web page with React. This will demonstrate how to use React components, JSX, and rendering.

1. **Set up your environment** (Refer to Chapter 1 for instructions on setting up the React development environment).

2. **Create a new component**: Start by creating a component that represents your webpage's header and content.

   Create a new file called Header.js in the src folder:

   javascript

   ```javascript
   import React from 'react';

   function Header() {
      return <h1>Welcome to My Simple React Page</h1>;
   }

   export default Header;
   ```

3. **Create another component** for your main content, such as an introductory paragraph.

Create a new file called `Content.js`:

javascript

```
import React from 'react';

function Content() {
    return <p>This is a simple React page to
demonstrate the basics of React components,
JSX, and rendering.</p>;
}

export default Content;
```

4. **Bring everything together in `App.js`:**

Modify `App.js` to import and render the `Header` and `Content` components:

javascript

```
import React from 'react';
import Header from './Header';
import Content from './Content';

function App() {
    return (
```

28

```
      <div>
        <Header />
        <Content />
      </div>
    );
}


export default App;
```

5. **Run your React app**:

Make sure your development server is running with npm
start. When you open your browser, you should see a
static web page with the heading "Welcome to My Simple
React Page" and the paragraph below it.

Conclusion

In this chapter, we've covered the fundamental concepts of React
components (functional and class-based), JSX, and rendering.
We've seen how components make up the building blocks of a
React application, how JSX allows us to write HTML-like syntax
within JavaScript, and how React handles rendering UI
components efficiently. The hands-on example demonstrated how
to create a simple static web page with React, setting the stage for
more dynamic, interactive web applications in the following
chapters.

Next, we will explore state management in React and how it allows you to create interactive components that respond to user input and data changes.

CHAPTER 3

MANAGING STATE IN REACT

What is State in React and Why Is It Important?

In React, **state** refers to the data or values that change over time and influence how a component renders. It is a core concept that allows React components to respond to user input, server responses, or any changes that occur during the lifecycle of the component.

State is **local** to a component, meaning that each component can have its own state. When state changes, React automatically re-renders the component, updating the user interface (UI) to reflect the new data. This makes React powerful for building interactive UIs where content dynamically changes without needing a full page reload.

For example, a user interacting with a form or a button could trigger a state change. As the state changes, React efficiently updates only the necessary parts of the UI, providing a smooth and responsive experience.

Why is state important in React?

- **Dynamic Behavior**: State allows your app to be interactive. It makes components capable of responding to user inputs and external events.

- **Reactivity**: React components automatically re-render when their state changes, ensuring the UI always reflects the current state.

- **Encapsulation**: Each component can manage its own state, keeping the logic isolated and reusable.

Using the `useState` Hook for Managing Local Component State

With the advent of **React Hooks** in version 16.8, managing state in functional components has become much simpler. The useState hook is the most commonly used hook for managing state in functional components. It allows you to add state to your functional components without the need for class-based components.

The useState hook returns an array with two values:

1. **The current state** value.
2. **A function** that allows you to update that state.

Here's the basic syntax of useState:

javascript

```
const          [state,          setState]          =
useState(initialState);
```

- `state` is the current value of the state.
- `setState` is the function used to update the state.
- `initialState` is the starting value of the state.

Example of using useState:

```
javascript

import React, { useState } from 'react';

function Counter() {
  // Declare a state variable 'count' with
initial value 0
  const [count, setCount] = useState(0);

  // Event handler to increment the count
  const increment = () => setCount(count + 1);

  return (
    <div>
      <h1>Counter: {count}</h1>
      <button
onClick={increment}>Increment</button>
    </div>
  );
}
```

```
export default Counter;
```

- In this example, `count` is the state variable, and `setCount` is the function used to update the state.
- When the user clicks the button, the `increment` function is called, updating the `count` state and causing the component to re-render with the new value.

State Management in Class Components

Before the introduction of hooks, React state management was handled in **class-based components** using the `this.state` object and the `this.setState()` method.

In a class component, you define the state within the constructor, and you use `this.setState()` to update it. React automatically re-renders the component whenever the state is updated using `setState`.

Here's an example of state management in a class component:

```javascript

import React, { Component } from 'react';

class Counter extends Component {
```

```
// Constructor to initialize state
constructor(props) {
  super(props);
  this.state = {
    count: 0,
  };
}

// Method to increment the count
increment = () => {
  this.setState({ count: this.state.count + 1
});
};

render() {
  return (
    <div>
      <h1>Counter: {this.state.count}</h1>
      <button
onClick={this.increment}>Increment</button>
    </div>
  );
}
}

export default Counter;
```

- In this example, this.state is used to define the initial state, and this.setState() is used to update the state.

35

- When the user clicks the "Increment" button, the `increment` method is invoked, which calls `setState` to update the `count` value and triggers a re-render of the component.

Although class components still work in React, **functional components with hooks** (such as `useState`) are now preferred for their simplicity and readability.

Example: A Counter App to Demonstrate State Management

Let's walk through an example of creating a simple **counter app** in React to demonstrate how state works, both in functional and class components.

1. Counter App with Functional Component (Using `useState`)

This version of the counter app uses a functional component and the `useState` hook to manage the state of the counter.

```javascript
import React, { useState } from 'react';

function Counter() {
    const [count, setCount] = useState(0);    // Initial state is set to 0
```

```
  // Increment function
  const increment = () => {
    setCount(count + 1);  // Update the state by
increasing the count by 1
  };

  // Decrement function
  const decrement = () => {
    setCount(count - 1);  // Update the state by
decreasing the count by 1
  };

  return (
    <div>
      <h1>Counter: {count}</h1>
      <button
onClick={increment}>Increment</button>
      <button
onClick={decrement}>Decrement</button>
    </div>
  );
}

export default Counter;
```

- In this example, we declare a state variable `count` initialized to 0 and provide `setCount` to update it.

- The `increment` function increases the `count`, and the `decrement` function decreases it when their respective buttons are clicked.

2. Counter App with Class Component (Using `this.state` and `this.setState`)

Here's the same counter app implemented with a class component:

javascript

```javascript
import React, { Component } from 'react';

class Counter extends Component {
  constructor(props) {
    super(props);
    this.state = { count: 0 };   // Initial state
  }

  increment = () => {
    this.setState({ count: this.state.count + 1
}); // Update state
  };

  decrement = () => {
    this.setState({ count: this.state.count - 1
}); // Update state
  };
```

```
render() {
    return (
      <div>
        <h1>Counter: {this.state.count}</h1>
        <button
onClick={this.increment}>Increment</button>
        <button
onClick={this.decrement}>Decrement</button>
      </div>
    );
  }
}

export default Counter;
```

- The functionality of the app remains the same, but this version uses class-based state management.
- `this.state` initializes the counter value, and `this.setState` updates the counter value when the buttons are clicked.

Conclusion

In this chapter, we've learned about **state** in React and its importance in managing dynamic and interactive UIs. We explored how to use the `useState` hook to manage local state in functional components, as well as how state is managed in class-based components using `this.state` and `this.setState`.

We also created a simple **counter app** to demonstrate state management, where clicking buttons updates the state and re-renders the component to reflect the changes.

Next, we will dive deeper into **handling user input and events** in React, exploring how to interact with users through forms, buttons, and other UI elements.

CHAPTER 4

HANDLING USER INPUT AND EVENTS

Understanding Events in React

In React, **events** are actions or occurrences that happen in the application, usually triggered by the user. These could be mouse clicks, key presses, form submissions, or even lifecycle events like component mounting. React provides a synthetic event system that wraps the browser's native event system, ensuring consistent behavior across different browsers.

Events in React are written in **camelCase** (e.g., onClick, onChange), rather than lowercase as in regular HTML. Additionally, React events do not use string values for event handlers but instead pass a function as the handler.

Example of a React event handler:

```javascript
<button onClick={handleClick}>Click Me</button>
```

- Here, `handleClick` is the function that will be executed when the user clicks the button.

React also normalizes events, which means that the event handling behavior is the same across different browsers, regardless of their quirks.

Event Object in React

When an event is triggered in React, an event object is automatically passed to the handler. This object contains details about the event, such as the type of event, the target element, and additional properties specific to the event type.

Example of an event object:

javascript

```
function handleClick(event) {
    console.log(event);
}
```

Here, `event` contains information about the event, such as the target element (`event.target`) and other useful properties like `event.type`.

Handling User Input Using Controlled and Uncontrolled Components

In React, user input can be managed using **controlled components** or **uncontrolled components**. Both approaches have their use cases, but controlled components are generally preferred due to their predictability and ease of maintenance.

Controlled Components

A **controlled component** is one where the React component manages the input value via the component's state. The input field's value is tied to the component's state, and any changes in the input field are handled through state updates.

In controlled components, the value of the input field is controlled by React, making it the "single source of truth."

Example of a controlled input component:

```javascript
import React, { useState } from 'react';

function ControlledForm() {
  const [value, setValue] = useState('');

  const handleChange = (event) => {
```

```
    setValue(event.target.value);    //    Update
state when user types
  };

  const handleSubmit = (event) => {
    event.preventDefault();
    console.log('Input    value    submitted:',
value);
  };

  return (
    <form onSubmit={handleSubmit}>
      <input
        type="text"
        value={value}
        onChange={handleChange}
        placeholder="Enter something"
      />
      <button type="submit">Submit</button>
    </form>
  );
}

export default ControlledForm;
```

- Here, the `input` field is controlled by React because its value is bound to the `value` state variable.
- Every time the user types something in the input field, the `handleChange` function is triggered, updating the

value state, which re-renders the input field with the new value.

Uncontrolled Components

An **uncontrolled component** is one where the input element's value is handled by the DOM itself rather than React. In uncontrolled components, React does not manage the value of the input field, and instead, you can access the current value directly using a **ref**.

Uncontrolled components are typically used when you need more direct access to the DOM or when integrating with non-React code.

Example of an uncontrolled component:

```javascript
import React, { useRef } from 'react';

function UncontrolledForm() {
  const inputRef = useRef();

  const handleSubmit = (event) => {
    event.preventDefault();
    console.log('Input     value     submitted:',
inputRef.current.value);
  };
```

```
return (
  <form onSubmit={handleSubmit}>
    <input      ref={inputRef}      type="text"
placeholder="Enter something" />
    <button type="submit">Submit</button>
  </form>
);
}
```

```
export default UncontrolledForm;
```

- In this example, the input field's value is not tied to the component's state. Instead, we use useRef to create a reference (inputRef) to the DOM element, and when the form is submitted, we access the current value using inputRef.current.value.

Example: Building a Form with User Input and Validation

Let's create a simple form with user input and validation. In this example, we will use a controlled component to manage the form's state and validate the input before submission.

We'll build a **sign-up form** with the following fields:

- Name (required)
- Email (required and valid format)

46

- Password (required, with a minimum length)

Form with Validation Example

javascript

```javascript
import React, { useState } from 'react';

function SignupForm() {
  const [formData, setFormData] = useState({
    name: '',
    email: '',
    password: '',
  });

  const [errors, setErrors] = useState({
    name: '',
    email: '',
    password: '',
  });

  const handleChange = (event) => {
    const { name, value } = event.target;
    setFormData((prevData) => ({
      ...prevData,
      [name]: value,
    }));
  };

  const validateForm = () => {
```

```
    const newErrors = {};
    if (!formData.name) newErrors.name = 'Name is
required';
    if (!formData.email) newErrors.email =
'Email is required';
    else                                        if
(!/\S+@\S+\.\S+/.test(formData.email))
newErrors.email = 'Email is invalid';
    if (!formData.password) newErrors.password =
'Password is required';
    else if (formData.password.length < 6)
newErrors.password = 'Password must be at least
6 characters long';

    setErrors(newErrors);
    return Object.keys(newErrors).length === 0;
// Return true if no errors
  };

  const handleSubmit = (event) => {
    event.preventDefault();
    if (validateForm()) {
      console.log('Form                    submitted
successfully:', formData);
    } else {
      console.log('Form     contains     errors:',
errors);
    }
  };
```

```jsx
  return (
    <form onSubmit={handleSubmit}>
      <div>
        <label>Name:</label>
        <input
          type="text"
          name="name"
          value={formData.name}
          onChange={handleChange}
          placeholder="Enter your name"
        />
        {errors.name && <p style={{ color: 'red'
}}>{errors.name}</p>}
      </div>

      <div>
        <label>Email:</label>
        <input
          type="email"
          name="email"
          value={formData.email}
          onChange={handleChange}
          placeholder="Enter your email"
        />
        {errors.email && <p style={{ color: 'red'
}}>{errors.email}</p>}
      </div>
```

```
<div>
  <label>Password:</label>
  <input
    type="password"
    name="password"
    value={formData.password}
    onChange={handleChange}
    placeholder="Enter your password"
  />
  {errors.password && <p style={{ color:
'red' }}>{errors.password}</p>}
</div>

  <button type="submit">Sign Up</button>
</form>
);
}


export default SignupForm;
```

Explanation:

- **State Management**: The form fields are controlled by React, and their values are stored in the `formData` state. We also have an `errors` state to keep track of any validation errors.
- **Validation**: When the user submits the form, we validate the inputs (name, email, and password). If any field is

empty or invalid, an error message is displayed below the corresponding field.

- **Form Submission**: If all fields pass validation, the form data is logged to the console. Otherwise, the errors are displayed, and the form is not submitted.

Key Points:

- The form fields are tied to React state, which is updated using the `handleChange` function whenever the user types.
- The `validateForm` function checks if the input values meet the requirements and updates the `errors` state accordingly.
- Conditional rendering is used to display error messages only if there are validation errors.

Conclusion

In this chapter, we've covered how to handle **user input and events** in React. You learned about **controlled and uncontrolled components** and how to manage input fields in React using state. Additionally, we explored how to build a simple form with validation, ensuring that users can only submit valid input. This is an essential skill for building interactive web applications.

In the next chapter, we will dive into **React's lifecycle methods and hooks**, exploring how to handle side effects and manage component behavior.

CHAPTER 5

REACT LIFECYCLE METHODS AND HOOKS

Introduction to Component Lifecycle Methods in Class Components

In React, a **component's lifecycle** refers to the series of stages a component goes through from its creation to its removal from the DOM. Lifecycle methods are hooks provided by React for executing code at specific points during a component's life. These methods are primarily used in **class-based components**.

There are three main phases in a component's lifecycle:

1. **Mounting**: When the component is being created and inserted into the DOM.
2. **Updating**: When the component's state or props change, causing the component to re-render.
3. **Unmounting**: When the component is removed from the DOM.

React provides specific lifecycle methods for each of these phases:

1. **Mounting Methods**:

o `constructor()`: Called before the component is mounted. It is used to initialize state and bind methods.

o `componentDidMount()`: Called once the component has been rendered and added to the DOM. It is commonly used for fetching data or setting up subscriptions.

2. **Updating Methods**:

o `shouldComponentUpdate()`: Determines whether the component should update when new props or state are received. It can optimize performance by preventing unnecessary re-renders.

o `componentDidUpdate()`: Called after the component has updated. This is useful for executing code in response to changes in props or state.

3. **Unmounting Method**:

o `componentWillUnmount()`: Called before the component is removed from the DOM. It is commonly used for cleaning up tasks like clearing timers, canceling network requests, or unsubscribing from services.

Here's an example using lifecycle methods in a class component:

javascript

```
import React, { Component } from 'react';

class LifecycleExample extends Component {
  constructor(props) {
    super(props);
    this.state = { data: null };
  }


  componentDidMount() {
    // This is called after the component is
mounted
    console.log('Component has been mounted');
    // Fetch data or perform side effects here

fetch('https://jsonplaceholder.typicode.com/pos
ts')
      .then((response) => response.json())
      .then((data) => this.setState({ data }));
  }


  componentDidUpdate(prevProps, prevState) {
    // Called after the component updates
    if (prevState.data !== this.state.data) {
      console.log('Component updated with new
data');
    }
  }
```

```
render() {
  const { data } = this.state;
  return (
    <div>
      <h1>Fetched Data</h1>
      <ul>
        {data
          ?    data.map((item)    =>    <li
key={item.id}>{item.title}</li>)
          : 'Loading...'}
      </ul>
    </div>
  );
}
}


export default LifecycleExample;
```

In this example:

- `componentDidMount()` is used to fetch data after the component is mounted.
- `componentDidUpdate()` logs a message every time the component re-renders due to a change in the `data` state.

Although lifecycle methods are essential in class-based components, React now offers a simpler and more powerful way to manage side effects and lifecycle behaviors in **functional components** with **React Hooks**.

Using React Hooks: useEffect for Side Effects

With the introduction of **React Hooks** in version 16.8, managing side effects (like data fetching, subscriptions, or manually changing the DOM) became much easier and more declarative. The useEffect hook is the most commonly used hook for handling side effects in **functional components**.

The useEffect hook is run after the render and is the replacement for many lifecycle methods in class components, such as componentDidMount, componentDidUpdate, and componentWillUnmount.

Syntax of useEffect:

javascript

```
useEffect(() => {
  // Code to run on component mount or update
}, [dependencies]);
```

- **First argument**: A function that contains the code to run. This function is executed after the component renders.
- **Second argument**: An array of dependencies. If any value in the array changes, the effect runs again. If the array is empty ([]), the effect runs only once after the initial render (like componentDidMount).

Example of `useEffect` for Side Effects:

javascript

```javascript
import React, { useState, useEffect } from 'react';

function DataFetchingComponent() {
  const [data, setData] = useState([]);
  const [loading, setLoading] = useState(true);

  useEffect(() => {
    // Fetch data when the component mounts

fetch('https://jsonplaceholder.typicode.com/posts')
      .then((response) => response.json())
      .then((data) => {
        setData(data); // Update state with the
fetched data
        setLoading(false); // Set loading to
false
      });
  }, []); // Empty dependency array means this
effect runs only once

  return (
    <div>
      <h1>Fetched Data</h1>
      {loading ? (
```

```
        <p>Loading...</p>
    ) : (
      <ul>
        {data.map((item) => (
          <li key={item.id}>{item.title}</li>
        ))}
      </ul>
    )}
  </div>
  );
}


export default DataFetchingComponent;
```

In this example:

- The useEffect hook is used to fetch data from an API when the component mounts. The empty dependency array [] ensures the effect runs only once after the initial render, similar to componentDidMount in class components.
- We use setState to update the data and loading states when the data is fetched.

How useEffect Works:

- If you don't pass a second argument (dependency array), the effect will run after every render, just like componentDidUpdate.

59

- If you pass an empty dependency array (`[]`), the effect runs only once after the initial render, like `componentDidMount`.
- If you pass an array of dependencies, the effect will run only when one of those dependencies changes.

Real-World Example: Fetching Data from an API and Updating the UI

Let's create a real-world example where we use **useEffect** to fetch data from an API and dynamically update the UI. We'll build a **user list** app that fetches user data from a public API.

javascript

```javascript
import React, { useState, useEffect } from 'react';

function UserList() {
  const [users, setUsers] = useState([]);
  const [loading, setLoading] = useState(true);

  useEffect(() => {
    // Fetch user data when the component mounts

fetch('https://jsonplaceholder.typicode.com/users')
```

```
    .then((response) => response.json())
    .then((data) => {
      setUsers(data);   // Update state with
user data
      setLoading(false);   // Set loading to
false once data is fetched
    });
  }, []);   // Empty dependency array means this
effect runs once

  return (
    <div>
      <h1>User List</h1>
      {loading ? (
        <p>Loading users...</p>
      ) : (
        <ul>
          {users.map((user) => (
            <li key={user.id}>
              {user.name} - {user.email}
            </li>
          ))}
        </ul>
      )}
    </div>
  );
}

export default UserList;
```

Explanation:

- We use the `useState` hook to manage the `users` and `loading` states.
- The `useEffect` hook fetches user data from the API when the component mounts. Once the data is fetched, we update the `users` state and set `loading` to `false`.
- If `loading` is `true`, we display a loading message; otherwise, we display the list of users.

This example illustrates how `useEffect` can be used to handle side effects, such as data fetching, in functional components. It also demonstrates how React automatically re-renders the component when the state changes, updating the UI with the fetched data.

Conclusion

In this chapter, we explored the **lifecycle methods** in class components and how they help manage component behavior during different phases of the lifecycle. We also learned how to use **React Hooks**, specifically `useEffect`, to handle side effects in functional components.

With `useEffect`, React simplifies handling tasks like fetching data, subscribing to services, and cleaning up resources, making it an essential tool for modern React development.

In the next chapter, we will dive into **advanced component patterns**, where we will explore higher-order components (HOCs) and render props, two powerful patterns that can help with reusability and composition in React applications.

CHAPTER 6

BUILDING REUSABLE COMPONENTS

Importance of Reusability in Component Design

One of the core principles in React development is **reusability**. A **reusable component** is a self-contained, modular piece of code that can be used in multiple places within your application without modification. Reusability promotes **maintainability** and **scalability** because developers can write components once and reuse them wherever necessary.

Why is reusability important?

1. **Consistency**: Reusable components ensure a consistent look and feel across your application. By using the same component in multiple places, you guarantee that the UI elements behave in the same way.

2. **Maintainability**: When a component is reused, it centralizes the logic. If you need to change the behavior or style of the component, you only have to do it once, making maintenance easier and reducing the likelihood of bugs.

3. **Efficiency**: Writing reusable components reduces duplication of code. This makes your codebase smaller, cleaner, and easier to understand.

4. **Scalability**: As your application grows, reusability becomes even more crucial. Instead of creating new components from scratch for every new feature, you can simply use or extend existing ones.

By breaking your application into reusable components, you promote **modularization**, making the development process more efficient and enabling faster iteration.

Passing Props to Components for Flexibility

In React, **props** (short for "properties") are how data is passed from one component to another. **Props** are the key mechanism for making components reusable and flexible.

1. **What are Props?**
   o Props are read-only properties that are passed down from a parent component to a child component.
   o They allow child components to receive dynamic data or behavior from their parents.

2. **Why Are Props Important for Reusability?**

o By passing props to components, you can control their content, style, and behavior from the parent, without modifying the component itself. This allows the component to be reused in different contexts with different values.

3. **How to Pass Props?** You pass props to a child component by including them as attributes when rendering the component. The child component can then access these props within its code.

Example of passing props:

javascript

```
function Greeting({ name }) {
  return <h1>Hello, {name}!</h1>;
}

function App() {
  return <Greeting name="John" />;
}
```

In this example:

- The Greeting component accepts a name prop, which is passed from the App component.
- When the App component is rendered, it passes "John" as the name prop to the Greeting component.

4. **Types of Props**:

  ○ **String**: Passing strings like text or URLs.

  ○ **Function**: Passing functions that child components can call.

  ○ **Array or Object**: Passing collections of data for more complex use cases.

Example: Building a Dynamic List Component That Can Be Reused in Multiple Places

Let's build a reusable **dynamic list component** that can display different types of lists based on the props passed to it. The component will be flexible enough to display any list of items (e.g., a list of tasks, users, or products), and you can customize how each item is rendered using props.

1. Defining the Dynamic List Component

We will define a component called `ItemList` that accepts two props:

- `items`: an array of data to be displayed in the list.
- `renderItem`: a function that defines how each item in the list should be rendered.

```javascript
```

```
import React from 'react';

// Dynamic list component
function ItemList({ items, renderItem }) {
  return (
    <ul>
      {items.map((item, index) => (
        <li key={index}>{renderItem(item)}</li>
      ))}
    </ul>
  );
}

export default ItemList;
```

In this component:

- The `items` prop is an array of data that will be passed to the component.
- The `renderItem` prop is a function that defines how to render each item. This allows us to customize the way each list item is displayed.

2. Using the `ItemList` Component

Now, let's use the `ItemList` component in different places in our app, passing different types of data and render functions.

1. **Example 1: Displaying a List of Tasks**

```javascript

import React from 'react';
import ItemList from './ItemList';

function App() {
  const tasks = [
    { id: 1, title: 'Learn React' },
    { id: 2, title: 'Build an app' },
    { id: 3, title: 'Deploy the app' }
  ];

  const renderTask = (task) => <span>{task.title}</span>;

  return (
    <div>
      <h1>Task List</h1>
      <ItemList items={tasks} renderItem={renderTask} />
    </div>
  );
}

export default App;
```

In this example:

- We pass an array of `tasks` as the `items` prop.

- We define a `renderTask` function that tells `ItemList` how to display each task's title.

2. **Example 2: Displaying a List of Users**

javascript

```javascript
import React from 'react';
import ItemList from './ItemList';

function App() {
  const users = [
    { id: 1, name: 'Alice', email: 'alice@example.com' },
    { id: 2, name: 'Bob', email: 'bob@example.com' },
    { id: 3, name: 'Charlie', email: 'charlie@example.com' }
  ];

  const renderUser = (user) => (
    <div>
      <h3>{user.name}</h3>
      <p>{user.email}</p>
    </div>
  );

  return (
    <div>
```

```
    <h1>User List</h1>
    <ItemList                 items={users}
renderItem={renderUser} />
  </div>
  );
}
```

```
export default App;
```

In this example:

- We pass an array of `users` as the `items` prop.
- We define a `renderUser` function that renders each user's name and email.

3. **Example 3: Displaying a List of Products**

```
javascript

import React from 'react';
import ItemList from './ItemList';

function App() {
  const products = [
    { id: 1, name: 'Laptop', price: '$999' },
    { id: 2, name: 'Smartphone', price: '$799' },
    { id: 3, name: 'Headphones', price: '$199' }
  ];

  const renderProduct = (product) => (
```

71

```
    <div>
      <h3>{product.name}</h3>
      <p>{product.price}</p>
    </div>
  );


  return (
    <div>
      <h1>Product List</h1>
      <ItemList                    items={products}
renderItem={renderProduct} />
    </div>
  );
}


export default App;
```

In this example:

- We pass an array of `products` as the `items` prop.
- We define a `renderProduct` function that renders each product's name and price.

Key Takeaways:

- The `ItemList` component is now reusable across the app for displaying different types of lists, whether it's tasks, users, or products.

- By passing different `renderItem` functions, you can customize how each list item is displayed.
- The `items` prop allows the component to be used with any type of data (arrays, objects, etc.).

Conclusion

In this chapter, we learned how to build **reusable components** in React. By passing data and rendering logic through **props**, we created a flexible component that could be used in different places with different data structures. We explored how to make our components more flexible and maintainable by allowing them to accept various inputs while keeping the component's logic intact.

This approach helps ensure that your React code is **modular** and **scalable**. In the next chapter, we will explore **conditional rendering** and how to work with lists in more complex applications, including advanced techniques for handling dynamic data.

CHAPTER 7

CONDITIONAL RENDERING AND LISTS

Using Conditional Rendering to Display Different UI Elements

Conditional rendering in React allows you to display different UI elements based on certain conditions. React does not have built-in concepts like `if` statements or ternary operators, but you can use standard JavaScript techniques like **if** statements, **ternary operators**, and **logical && operators** to determine what to render.

Common Methods of Conditional Rendering:

1. **Using if-else Statements**: You can use JavaScript's `if` statement to check conditions and decide what to render.

   Example:

   ```javascript
   javascript

   function Greeting({ isLoggedIn }) {
     if (isLoggedIn) {
       return <h1>Welcome back, User!</h1>;
   ```

```
} else {
    return <h1>Please log in.</h1>;
}
}
```

In this example, if isLoggedIn is true, the message "Welcome back, User!" is displayed. Otherwise, the message "Please log in" is shown.

2. **Using Ternary Operator**: The ternary operator is a shorthand for if-else and can be used directly in JSX to make your code more concise.

Example:

javascript

```
function Greeting({ isLoggedIn }) {
    return isLoggedIn ? <h1>Welcome back,
User!</h1> : <h1>Please log in.</h1>;
}
```

This accomplishes the same as the previous example but in a more compact way.

3. **Using the Logical AND (&&) Operator**: The logical && operator can be used to render a component only if the condition is true. If the condition is false, nothing is rendered.

75

Example:

```
javascript
```

```
function Notification({ hasMessages }) {
    return (
      <div>
        {hasMessages && <p>You have new
messages!</p>}
      </div>
    );
}
```

Here, the message will only be displayed if hasMessages is true. If hasMessages is false, nothing will be rendered.

When to Use Conditional Rendering?

- Conditional rendering is useful when you need to render different content based on user actions, such as logging in, submitting a form, or receiving new data from an API.
- It is a powerful way to manage UI changes without having to modify the entire structure of your components.

Rendering Lists of Data Dynamically with .map ()

In React, rendering lists of data is a common task, and the .map()
function is typically used to iterate over an array and render a list
of elements. The .map() method is a JavaScript array method that
creates a new array by applying a function to each element in the
original array.

How .map() Works in React:

The .map() method returns a new array with the results of calling
the provided function on every element in the original array. It's
used for rendering lists of elements in React.

Example:

javascript

```
const items = ['Apple', 'Banana', 'Orange'];

function FruitList() {
  return (
    <ul>
      {items.map((item, index) => (
        <li key={index}>{item}</li>
      ))}
    </ul>
  );
}
```

In this example:

- We have an array `items` containing fruit names.
- We use `.map()` to iterate over the `items` array and render each item inside an `<li>` element.
- **key** is an important prop in React when rendering lists. It helps React identify which items have changed, been added, or removed, improving performance during re-renders.

Best Practices for Rendering Lists:

1. Always provide a unique `key` prop when rendering lists to help React optimize rendering.
2. Avoid using array indices as keys if the order of items might change, as this could lead to bugs during re-rendering.
3. If you're rendering a list of objects, make sure to pass a unique property (like an `id`) as the key.

Example: Building a To-Do List App with Dynamic Rendering

Let's create a simple **To-Do List app** where users can add tasks, mark them as completed, and remove them. We'll use **conditional rendering** and `.map()` to dynamically render the list of tasks.

Step 1: Set Up the To-Do List Component

javascript

```javascript
import React, { useState } from 'react';

function TodoApp() {
  const [tasks, setTasks] = useState([]);
  const [newTask, setNewTask] = useState('');

  // Add a new task to the list
  const addTask = () => {
    if (newTask.trim()) {
      setTasks([...tasks,  {  id:  Date.now(),
text: newTask, isCompleted: false }]);
      setNewTask('');
    }
  };

  // Toggle task completion
  const toggleTask = (id) => {
    setTasks(tasks.map(task =>
      task.id === id ? { ...task, isCompleted:
!task.isCompleted } : task
    ));
  };

  // Remove a task from the list
  const removeTask = (id) => {
```

```
    setTasks(tasks.filter(task  =>  task.id  !==
id));
  };


  return (
    <div>
      <h1>To-Do List</h1>

      {/* Input and Button to Add Task */}
      <input
        type="text"
        value={newTask}
        onChange={(e)                              =>
setNewTask(e.target.value)}
        placeholder="Enter a new task"
      />
      <button           onClick={addTask}>Add
Task</button>

      {/* List of Tasks */}
      <ul>
        {tasks.length > 0 ? (
          tasks.map((task) => (
            <li key={task.id}>
              <span
                style={{          textDecoration:
task.isCompleted ? 'line-through' : 'none' }}
                onClick={()                        =>
toggleTask(task.id)}
```

```
            >
                {task.text}
            </span>
            <button        onClick={()        =>
removeTask(task.id)}>Remove</button>
        </li>
      ))
    ) : (
        <p>No tasks to display</p>
      )}
    </ul>
  </div>
);
}


export default TodoApp;
```

Explanation:

- **State Management**:
  - o tasks: An array of tasks, each containing an id, text, and a boolean isCompleted property.
  - o newTask: The text input that holds the value of the new task to be added.
- **Adding Tasks**: The addTask function adds a new task to the tasks array when the "Add Task" button is clicked.
- **Toggling Completion**: The toggleTask function toggles the isCompleted property of a task. If the task is completed, it will have a strikethrough style.

81

- **Removing Tasks**: The `removeTask` function removes a task from the list by filtering out the task with the corresponding `id`.
- **Conditional Rendering**: The task list is rendered dynamically using `.map()`. If there are no tasks, a message "No tasks to display" is shown.

Key Concepts Covered:

1. **Conditional Rendering**: We used conditional rendering to display a message when there are no tasks (`tasks.length > 0 ?`).
2. **Rendering Lists**: The list of tasks is dynamically rendered using `.map()` to iterate over the `tasks` array and display each task.
3. **Event Handlers**: We created event handlers for adding, toggling, and removing tasks. Each task item is clickable to toggle its completion status.

Conclusion

In this chapter, we covered **conditional rendering** and how it can be used to display different UI elements based on certain conditions. We also explored how to **render lists dynamically** using the `.map()` method, which is essential for working with arrays of data in React.

We built a simple **To-Do List app** where tasks can be added, marked as completed, and removed, showcasing how conditional rendering and `.map()` work together to create dynamic and interactive user interfaces.

In the next chapter, we will dive into **advanced component patterns**, where we will explore higher-order components (HOCs) and render props, two powerful techniques for reusing logic across components in a React application.

CHAPTER 8

ADVANCED COMPONENT PATTERNS

Higher-Order Components (HOCs) and Their Usage

A **Higher-Order Component (HOC)** is a pattern in React that allows you to reuse component logic. HOCs are not part of the React API but are a pattern used to share common behavior between multiple components. An HOC is a function that takes a component and returns a new component with additional props or functionality.

The key idea behind HOCs is that they allow you to **enhance or modify the behavior** of a component without directly modifying the original component.

Why Use Higher-Order Components?

1. **Code Reusability**: By extracting common logic into an HOC, you avoid duplicating code across multiple components.

2. **Cross-Cutting Concerns**: HOCs are useful for implementing features that apply to multiple components, such as authentication checks, logging, data fetching, etc.

3. **Separation of Concerns**: HOCs help separate logic from UI rendering, making components easier to maintain.

How HOCs Work:

An HOC is a function that accepts a component as an argument and returns a new component. The new component can add additional props, wrap the original component, or modify its behavior.

Example of an HOC:

javascript

```javascript
import React from 'react';

// HOC that adds logging functionality
function withLogging(WrappedComponent) {
  return function (props) {
    console.log('Component       rendered       with
props:', props);
    return <WrappedComponent {...props} />;
  };
}


function Button(props) {
```

```
  return <button>{props.label}</button>;
}


// Enhance the Button component with logging
functionality
const ButtonWithLogging = withLogging(Button);


function App() {
  return <ButtonWithLogging label="Click Me" />;
}


export default App;
```

In this example:

- withLogging is an HOC that adds logging functionality to any component passed into it.
- ButtonWithLogging is the result of applying withLogging to the Button component. This enhanced component logs props every time it is rendered.

Key Points About HOCs:

- HOCs don't modify the original component; they return a new component with enhanced functionality.
- HOCs are typically used for cross-cutting concerns like **authentication**, **authorization**, **data fetching**, or **handling lifecycle events**.

- An HOC does not modify the component's internal state or behavior but adds additional props or logic to the component.

Render Props Pattern in React

The **render props** pattern is another technique used to share code between components. It involves passing a function (a "render prop") to a component that returns JSX. This pattern enables components to delegate the rendering of part of their UI to another function, allowing for greater flexibility and reusability.

Why Use Render Props?

1. **Dynamic Rendering**: It enables a component to delegate the rendering of its children, making it more flexible and reusable in different scenarios.
2. **State Sharing**: Render props allow components to share state and behavior without explicitly passing it as props, improving modularity.
3. **Flexibility**: By passing functions as props, components can dynamically adjust their content or behavior based on the input.

How the Render Props Pattern Works:

In the render props pattern, a component accepts a function as a prop, and this function is used to render the component's UI.

Example:

```javascript

import React, { useState } from 'react';

// Component that provides state via a render
prop
function MouseTracker({ render }) {
  const [mousePosition, setMousePosition] =
useState({ x: 0, y: 0 });

  const handleMouseMove = (event) => {
    setMousePosition({
      x: event.clientX,
      y: event.clientY,
    });
  };

  return (
    <div style={{ height: '100vh' }}
onMouseMove={handleMouseMove}>
      {render(mousePosition)}
    </div>
```

```
  );
}

function App() {
  return (
    <div>
      <h1>Move the Mouse!</h1>
      <MouseTracker
        render={({ x, y }) => <h2>The mouse is at
({x}, {y})</h2>}
      />
    </div>
  );
}

export default App;
```

In this example:

- The `MouseTracker` component accepts a `render` function as a prop. This function will be called with the current mouse position and is used to render the UI.
- The `App` component provides the `render` function to `MouseTracker`, which dynamically renders the mouse coordinates on the screen.

Key Points About Render Props:

- The render function is typically passed as a prop to the component that will control part of its rendering.
- Render props enable components to share state or behavior without tightly coupling components together.
- This pattern is useful for creating highly reusable components, such as handling mouse or keyboard events, animations, or form validations.

Real-World Example: Enhancing a Button Component with Advanced Patterns

Now, let's apply both **Higher-Order Components** and the **Render Props** pattern to enhance a button component with more advanced behavior, such as logging clicks and handling dynamic content.

1. Button Component with HOC for Logging

We'll start by creating a button component and using an HOC to add logging functionality.

javascript

import React from 'react';

```
// HOC to log button clicks
function withLogging(WrappedComponent) {
  return function (props) {
    const handleClick = () => {
      console.log('Button clicked!');
      if (props.onClick) {
        props.onClick();
      }
    };

    return <WrappedComponent {...props}
onClick={handleClick} />;
  };
}


function Button({ label, onClick }) {
  return                                 <button
onClick={onClick}>{label}</button>;
}


const ButtonWithLogging = withLogging(Button);

function App() {
  return <ButtonWithLogging label="Click Me" />;
}


export default App;
```

Here, the `withLogging` HOC enhances the `Button` component, adding logging functionality when the button is clicked. The `ButtonWithLogging` component will log the click event each time it's triggered.

2. Button Component with Render Props for Dynamic Content

Now, let's enhance the button to accept dynamic content using the **render props** pattern. This will allow us to change the button's content or behavior based on the data passed via the render prop.

```javascript
import React from 'react';

function ButtonWithRenderProps({ render }) {
  return <button>{render()}</button>;
}

function App() {
  return (
    <div>
      <h1>Render Props Example</h1>
      <ButtonWithRenderProps
        render={() => (
          <span>
            <strong>Click me!</strong>
          </span>
        )}
```

```
    />
  </div>
);
}
```

```
export default App;
```

In this example:

- The `ButtonWithRenderProps` component accepts a `render` function, which allows dynamic content to be passed in.
- Inside `App`, the `render` function is used to display custom content (`Click me!` wrapped in a `strong` tag).

3. Combining HOC and Render Props

We can combine both the **HOC** and **render props** pattern to create a button that logs clicks and also renders dynamic content.

```javascript
import React, { useState } from 'react';

// HOC to log button clicks
function withLogging(WrappedComponent) {
  return function (props) {
    const handleClick = () => {
      console.log('Button clicked!');
```

```
    if (props.onClick) {
      props.onClick();
    }
  };

    return        <WrappedComponent        {...props}
onClick={handleClick} />;
  };
}

function ButtonWithRenderProps({ render, onClick
}) {
  return                          . <button
onClick={onClick}>{render()}</button>;
}

const          ButtonWithLogging          =
withLogging(ButtonWithRenderProps);

function App() {
  const [message, setMessage] = useState('Click
me to log the event!');

  return (
    <div>
      <h1>Combined   HOC   and   Render   Props
Example</h1>
      <ButtonWithLogging
        render={() => <span>{message}</span>}
```

```
      onClick={() => setMessage('Thank you for
clicking!')}
    />
  </div>
);
}
```

```
export default App;
```

In this combined example:

- We use the **withLogging HOC** to add click logging functionality.
- We also use the **render props pattern** to allow dynamic content (`message`) to be passed into the button.
- Clicking the button changes the message and logs the click.

Conclusion

In this chapter, we explored two powerful advanced component patterns in React: **Higher-Order Components (HOCs)** and the **Render Props** pattern.

- **HOCs** are useful for reusing logic and enhancing the functionality of components without modifying their code directly. We saw how to apply an HOC to log button clicks.

- **Render Props** allow for greater flexibility by passing a function as a prop to dynamically render content. We demonstrated how to create a button with dynamic content using render props.

Both patterns are valuable tools in React development, enabling more flexible and reusable components. In the next chapter, we will explore **context and state management**, diving into how to share data across components without prop drilling.

CHAPTER 9

REACT ROUTER FOR NAVIGATION

Setting Up React Router for Single-Page Applications (SPAs)

In React, **React Router** is a library that allows you to implement **client-side routing** in your application, enabling navigation between different views or pages without the need to reload the page. This is crucial for creating **Single-Page Applications (SPAs)**, where the entire application is loaded initially, and navigation is handled dynamically using JavaScript.

Installing React Router

To start using React Router in your project, you first need to install the `react-router-dom` package, which is the library for React Router in web applications.

Run the following command in your project directory:

```bash
npm install react-router-dom
```

After installation, you'll be able to import and use React Router components in your React app.

Basic Setup of React Router

1. **Importing React Router Components**: To use React Router in your app, you need to import the necessary components like BrowserRouter, Route, and Switch.

   javascript

   ```
   import { BrowserRouter as Router, Route,
   Switch } from 'react-router-dom';
   ```

2. **Using Router**: The Router component is the top-level component that wraps your entire application, enabling routing functionality.

3. **Defining Routes**: The Route component is used to define a specific route and the corresponding component to render when that route is visited.

4. **Switching Between Routes**: The Switch component ensures that only one Route is rendered at a time.

Basic Example of React Router Setup:

javascript

```
import React from 'react';
```

```
import { BrowserRouter as Router, Route, Switch
} from 'react-router-dom';

function Home() {
  return <h2>Home Page</h2>;
}

function About() {
  return <h2>About Page</h2>;
}

function Contact() {
  return <h2>Contact Page</h2>;
}

function App() {
  return (
    <Router>
      <div>
        <nav>
          <ul>
            <li>
              <a href="/">Home</a>
            </li>
            <li>
              <a href="/about">About</a>
            </li>
            <li>
              <a href="/contact">Contact</a>
```

```
          </li>
        </ul>
      </nav>

      <Switch>
        <Route exact path="/" component={Home}
/>
        <Route path="/about" component={About}
/>
        <Route              path="/contact"
component={Contact} />
      </Switch>
    </div>
  </Router>
 );
}

export default App;
```

In this example:

- We have a simple app with three pages: Home, About, and Contact.
- The `Router` component wraps the entire app, enabling routing.
- The `Route` components define the paths (`/`, `/about`, `/contact`) and the components to render when these paths are visited.

- The `Switch` component ensures that only one route is rendered at a time.

Important Notes:

- The `exact` prop in the `/` route ensures that the Home component only renders when the URL is exactly `/` (not `/about` or `/contact`).
- The links in the navigation (`<a href="/">`) can be replaced with React Router's `<Link>` component for client-side navigation (without page reloads).

Working with Routes, Parameters, and Nested Routing

React Router allows you to work with dynamic routes (using **parameters**) and create **nested routes** for complex UI structures.

1. Route Parameters

You can pass dynamic values in the URL using **route parameters**. Route parameters are specified in the URL path using a colon (:).

Example:

```
javascript
```

```
function UserProfile({ match }) {
  return   <h2>User   Profile   for   User   ID:
{match.params.userId}</h2>;
}

function App() {
  return (
    <Router>
      <Switch>
        <Route                    path="/user/:userId"
component={UserProfile} />
      </Switch>
    </Router>
  );
}
```

In this example:

- The route /user/:userId defines a dynamic route
  where :userId is a route parameter.
- Inside the UserProfile component, we access the
  userId parameter using match.params.userId.

To navigate to this route, the URL would look like /user/123,
and UserProfile will display "User Profile for User ID: 123".

2. Nested Routing

Nested routes allow you to create layouts with sub-routes. For example, a dashboard may have multiple sections such as settings, profile, and notifications. These sections can be rendered as nested routes inside the main dashboard component.

Example of nested routes:

```javascript
import React from 'react';
import { BrowserRouter as Router, Route, Switch
} from 'react-router-dom';

function Dashboard() {
  return (
    <div>
      <h2>Dashboard</h2>
      <nav>
        <ul>
          <li><a
href="/dashboard/settings">Settings</a></li>
          <li><a
href="/dashboard/profile">Profile</a></li>
        </ul>
      </nav>
      <Switch>
```

```jsx
        <Route          path="/dashboard/settings"
component={Settings} />
        <Route           path="/dashboard/profile"
component={Profile} />
      </Switch>
    </div>
  );
}

function Settings() {
  return <h3>Settings Page</h3>;
}

function Profile() {
  return <h3>Profile Page</h3>;
}

function App() {
  return (
    <Router>
      <Switch>
        <Route               path="/dashboard"
component={Dashboard} />
      </Switch>
    </Router>
  );
}

export default App;
```

In this example:

- We have a main `Dashboard` component that contains links to two nested routes (`/dashboard/settings` and `/dashboard/profile`).
- The `Switch` inside `Dashboard` handles these nested routes, rendering `Settings` or `Profile` based on the URL.

Example: Building a Multi-Page App with Navigation Between Pages

Let's build a **multi-page application** that demonstrates navigation between different pages using React Router. We will create an app with the following pages:

- Home
- About
- Services
- Contact

Each page will be rendered based on the route, and we'll have a simple navigation bar to switch between them.

```javascript
import React from 'react';
```

```
import { BrowserRouter as Router, Route, Switch,
Link } from 'react-router-dom';

function Home() {
  return <h2>Home Page</h2>;
}

function About() {
  return <h2>About Us</h2>;
}

function Services() {
  return <h2>Our Services</h2>;
}

function Contact() {
  return <h2>Contact Us</h2>;
}

function App() {
  return (
    <Router>
      <div>
        <nav>
          <ul>
            <li><Link to="/">Home</Link></li>
            <li><Link
to="/about">About</Link></li>
```

```
                <li><Link
to="/services">Services</Link></li>
                <li><Link
to="/contact">Contact</Link></li>
            </ul>
        </nav>

        <Switch>
            <Route exact path="/" component={Home}
/>
            <Route path="/about" component={About}
/>
            <Route              path="/services"
component={Services} />
            <Route              path="/contact"
component={Contact} />
        </Switch>
    </div>
  </Router>
  );
}

export default App;
```

In this example:

- We have four pages: Home, About, Services, and
  Contact, each associated with its route.

- The navigation links (`<Link>`) allow the user to navigate between these pages without reloading the browser.
- The `Switch` component ensures that only one route is rendered at a time.
- The `exact` prop on the Home route ensures that it is only rendered when the URL is exactly `/`.

Key Points:

- The `Link` component is used instead of `<a>` to avoid full-page reloads, making the app faster by only updating the parts of the UI that have changed.
- `exact` ensures that the Home page only renders on the exact `/` path.

Conclusion

In this chapter, we explored **React Router**, which is a powerful library for handling navigation in single-page applications (SPAs). We covered:

- **Setting up React Router** to enable client-side routing.
- **Working with routes**, including defining static routes, using route parameters, and nesting routes for complex UI structures.

- We demonstrated how to create a **multi-page app** with navigation between different pages.

React Router is an essential tool for building complex, dynamic SPAs, providing developers with flexibility in managing navigation and rendering components efficiently. In the next chapter, we will explore **state management** in React using context and **Redux** for handling more complex application state.

CHAPTER 10

FORM HANDLING AND VALIDATION

Controlled vs Uncontrolled Form Elements

In React, form elements can be classified as either **controlled** or **uncontrolled**, depending on how their values are managed.

1. Controlled Form Elements

A **controlled form element** is one where the form data (like the value of an input field) is controlled by React's state. This means that the state of the form element is bound to the component's state, and the state is updated whenever the user interacts with the form.

In controlled components, the input field's value is always derived from the component's state, making it the **single source of truth**.

Key Characteristics of Controlled Components:

- The value of the input is stored in React state.
- You can use event handlers like `onChange` to handle changes to the input field.

- It offers a better way to manipulate or validate the input since you control the form's data in state.

Example of Controlled Component:

```javascript
import React, { useState } from 'react';

function ControlledForm() {
  const [email, setEmail] = useState('');

  const handleChange = (event) => {
    setEmail(event.target.value); // Update the
email state as the user types
  };

  const handleSubmit = (event) => {
    event.preventDefault();
    console.log('Email submitted:', email);
  };

  return (
    <form onSubmit={handleSubmit}>
      <input
        type="email"
        value={email}
        onChange={handleChange}
        placeholder="Enter your email"
```

```
      />
      <button type="submit">Submit</button>
    </form>
  );
}
```

```
export default ControlledForm;
```

In this example:

- The value of the input is controlled by the `email` state.
- Whenever the user types in the input field, the `handleChange` function updates the `email` state.

2. Uncontrolled Form Elements

An **uncontrolled form element** is one where the form data is handled by the DOM itself rather than React. The input field's value is not tied to the component's state, and you can use a **ref** to access the input value directly.

Key Characteristics of Uncontrolled Components:

- The form data is managed by the DOM.
- You can access the value using refs instead of state.
- Uncontrolled components are more suitable when integrating with non-React libraries or when you don't need to manage the state of the form.

Example of Uncontrolled Component:

```javascript
import React, { useRef } from 'react';

function UncontrolledForm() {
  const emailRef = useRef();

  const handleSubmit = (event) => {
    event.preventDefault();
    console.log('Email                submitted:',
emailRef.current.value);
  };

  return (
    <form onSubmit={handleSubmit}>
      <input
        type="email"
        ref={emailRef}
        placeholder="Enter your email"
      />
      <button type="submit">Submit</button>
    </form>
  );
}

export default UncontrolledForm;
```

In this example:

- The value of the input field is accessed using a `ref` (`emailRef`).
- The input's value is not tied to the component's state, and React doesn't manage it directly.

Validating Form Input and Providing User Feedback

Validating form input is essential for ensuring that the data entered by users is correct and meets the necessary criteria before it is submitted. Validation can be done on the client side (in the browser) and on the server side, but client-side validation is often used to give immediate feedback to users.

Basic Form Validation

You can validate form input in React by using the following techniques:

1. **Required Fields**: Ensure that required fields are filled in.
2. **Pattern Matching**: Ensure that data matches a certain pattern (e.g., valid email format).
3. **Min/Max Length**: Ensure that the input length is within a specific range.

Example of Email Validation:

```
javascript
```

```jsx
import React, { useState } from 'react';

function SignUpForm() {
  const [email, setEmail] = useState('');
  const [error, setError] = useState('');

  const handleChange = (event) => {
    setEmail(event.target.value);
  };

  const validateEmail = (email) => {
    const emailPattern = /^[a-zA-Z0-9._-]+@[a-zA-Z0-9.-]+\.[a-zA-Z]{2,6}$/;
    return emailPattern.test(email);
  };

  const handleSubmit = (event) => {
    event.preventDefault();
    if (!validateEmail(email)) {
      setError('Please enter a valid email address.');
    } else {
      setError('');
      console.log('Form submitted with email:', email);
    }
  };
```

```
  return (
    <form onSubmit={handleSubmit}>
      <input
        type="email"
        value={email}
        onChange={handleChange}
        placeholder="Enter your email"
      />
      {error && <p style={{ color: 'red'
}}>{error}</p>}
      <button type="submit">Submit</button>
    </form>
  );
}

export default SignUpForm;
```

In this example:

- The `validateEmail` function checks if the email entered by the user matches the standard email pattern using a regular expression.
- If the email is invalid, an error message is displayed below the input field.
- If the email is valid, the form is submitted, and the email is logged.

Feedback to Users

It's important to provide **real-time feedback** to users as they interact with the form. This can be done using:

- Error messages when validation fails.
- Success messages when the form is correctly filled out.
- Input styling (e.g., red borders for invalid fields).

Real-World Example: Creating a Sign-Up Form with Validation and Error Messages

Let's build a **sign-up form** that includes validation for required fields and checks if the email is in the correct format. We'll also provide user feedback when there's an error.

```javascript
import React, { useState } from 'react';

function SignUpForm() {
  const [email, setEmail] = useState('');
  const [password, setPassword] = useState('');
  const [error, setError] = useState('');

  const handleEmailChange = (event) => {
    setEmail(event.target.value);
  };
```

117

```
const handlePasswordChange = (event) => {
  setPassword(event.target.value);
};


const validateForm = () => {
  if (!email || !password) {
    return 'All fields are required.';
  }
  const emailPattern = /^[a-zA-Z0-9._-]+@[a-
zA-Z0-9.-]+\.[a-zA-Z]{2,6}$/;
  if (!emailPattern.test(email)) {
    return 'Please enter a valid email
address.';
  }
  if (password.length < 6) {
    return 'Password must be at least 6
characters long.';
  }
  return '';
};


const handleSubmit = (event) => {
  event.preventDefault();
  const validationError = validateForm();
  if (validationError) {
    setError(validationError);
  } else {
    setError('');
```

```
    console.log('Form submitted:', { email,
password });
  }
};


return (
  <form onSubmit={handleSubmit}>
    <div>
      <label>Email:</label>
      <input
        type="email"
        value={email}
        onChange={handleEmailChange}
        placeholder="Enter your email"
      />
    </div>
    <div>
      <label>Password:</label>
      <input
        type="password"
        value={password}
        onChange={handlePasswordChange}
        placeholder="Enter your password"
      />
    </div>
    {error && <p style={{ color: 'red'
}}>{error}</p>}
    <button type="submit">Sign Up</button>
  </form>
```

```
    );
}
```

```
export default SignUpForm;
```

Explanation:

1. **State Management**: We manage the state for `email`, `password`, and `error` using the `useState` hook.
2. **Form Validation**:
   - o The `validateForm` function checks if all fields are filled, validates the email format, and ensures the password is at least 6 characters long.
   - o If any validation fails, an error message is displayed.
3. **User Feedback**: Error messages are displayed dynamically below the form fields if validation fails.
4. **Form Submission**: If validation passes, the form is "submitted" (in this case, logged to the console).

Conclusion

In this chapter, we explored how to handle forms and perform validation in React. We discussed:

120

- **Controlled vs uncontrolled form elements**, emphasizing the benefits of controlled components for managing form data.
- **Validating form input** using regular expressions and basic checks, as well as providing user feedback with error messages.
- A **real-world example** of creating a sign-up form with email and password validation.

Form handling and validation are essential for ensuring that user input is correct before submission. In the next chapter, we will explore **state management** with **React Context** and **Redux**, which will help manage complex application state across multiple components.

CHAPTER 11

MANAGING STATE WITH CONTEXT API

Introduction to the Context API for Global State Management

The **Context API** in React is a powerful feature that allows you to manage global state and share data between components without the need to explicitly pass props down through every level of the component tree. This is especially useful when you have deeply nested components or need to manage global settings like themes, user authentication, or language preferences across the entire app.

Before the Context API, managing global state often meant passing data from parent to child components through **prop drilling** (i.e., passing props through many layers of components), which could become cumbersome and difficult to maintain. The Context API provides a cleaner and more efficient way to manage such global data, reducing the need for prop drilling.

What is the Context API?

- **Context Provider**: The component that provides the data to the component tree.
- **Context Consumer**: The component that consumes the provided data.
- **useContext Hook**: A hook that allows functional components to access the nearest value of a Context in the component tree.

Key Concepts:

1. **Provider**: The `Context.Provider` component allows you to pass a value down the component tree, making it available to any component that subscribes to the context.
2. **Consumer**: The `useContext` hook or `Context.Consumer` component allows components to access the context value and react to changes.

Passing Data Between Components Without Prop Drilling

In React, when you need to pass data to deeply nested components, you typically have to pass it down through every intermediate component (prop drilling). However, with the Context API, you can skip the intermediary steps and directly provide data to any component in the tree.

How to Use Context API:

1. **Create a Context**: First, you create a context using `React.createContext()`.

2. **Provide the Context Value**: Use the `Provider` component to provide the context value at a higher level in the component tree.

3. **Consume the Context Value**: Use the `useContext` hook or `Context.Consumer` to consume the context value in any child component.

Here's how you can use the Context API to share data between components.

Example: Creating a Theme Toggler with Context API

In this example, we will create a simple **theme toggler** that allows users to switch between a **light** and **dark** theme. We will use the Context API to manage the theme globally across the app, so that it can be accessed by any component without prop drilling.

Step 1: Create the Context

First, create a context that will hold the theme state.

javascript

```
import React, { createContext, useState } from
'react';

// Create a Context for the theme
const ThemeContext = createContext();

export const ThemeProvider = ({ children }) => {
  const [theme, setTheme] = useState('light'); //
Default theme is light

  // Function to toggle between light and dark
theme
  const toggleTheme = () => {
    setTheme(theme === 'light' ? 'dark' :
'light');
  };

  return (
    <ThemeContext.Provider    value={{    theme,
toggleTheme }}>
      {children}
    </ThemeContext.Provider>
  );
};

export default ThemeContext;
```

Here:

- We create a ThemeContext using createContext().

- The ThemeProvider component provides the theme state and the toggleTheme function to the component tree.
- The value prop of Provider contains the data (the current theme and the toggleTheme function) that will be accessible to all child components.

Step 2: Consuming the Context in Components

Now, let's create components that consume the context and allow users to toggle between themes.

1. ThemedComponent (UI that changes based on theme):

javascript

```javascript
import React, { useContext } from 'react';
import ThemeContext from './ThemeContext';

const ThemedComponent = () => {
  const { theme } = useContext(ThemeContext); // Access the theme from context

  return (
    <div style={{ background: theme === 'light' ? '#fff' : '#333', color: theme === 'light' ? '#000' : '#fff', padding: '20px' }}>
      <h1>{theme === 'light' ? 'Light Theme' : 'Dark Theme'}</h1>
```

```
    </div>
  );
};
```

```
export default ThemedComponent;
```

- Here, we use the `useContext` hook to get the current theme from the `ThemeContext`. The background color and text color change based on the theme value.

2. ThemeToggler (Button to toggle between themes):

javascript

```
import React, { useContext } from 'react';
import ThemeContext from './ThemeContext';

const ThemeToggler = () => {
  const { toggleTheme } =
useContext(ThemeContext); // Get the toggleTheme
function from context

  return <button onClick={toggleTheme}>Toggle
Theme</button>;
};
```

```
export default ThemeToggler;
```

- The `ThemeToggler` component accesses the `toggleTheme` function from the context and toggles the theme when the button is clicked.

Step 3: Wrapping the App with the ThemeProvider

Finally, we need to wrap the entire app with the `ThemeProvider` so that the theme context is accessible in the entire component tree.

javascript

```javascript
import React from 'react';
import { ThemeProvider } from './ThemeContext';
import ThemedComponent from './ThemedComponent';
import ThemeToggler from './ThemeToggler';

function App() {
  return (
    <ThemeProvider>
      <ThemedComponent />
      <ThemeToggler />
    </ThemeProvider>
  );
}

export default App;
```

Here:

- The `ThemeProvider` is used to wrap the components that need access to the theme context.
- The `ThemedComponent` displays the UI based on the current theme, and the `ThemeToggler` button allows users to toggle the theme.

Key Benefits of Using Context API

- **Avoid Prop Drilling**: The Context API eliminates the need to pass data through every intermediate component, making the code cleaner and easier to maintain.
- **Global State**: It's a convenient way to manage global state, such as user authentication status, theme, language settings, etc.
- **Easier State Sharing**: It's easier to share state between distant components in the tree without managing complex state-passing logic.

Conclusion

In this chapter, we introduced the **Context API** for global state management in React. The Context API provides a simple way to manage and share state across components without needing to pass props through every level of the component tree.

We used the Context API to build a **theme toggler** that allows switching between light and dark themes. This example demonstrated how to:

- Create and provide context with the `Provider` component.
- Consume context using the `useContext` hook.
- Simplify global state management and avoid prop drilling.

The Context API is ideal for simpler state management, but for more complex scenarios (such as managing state across multiple components with many updates), you might need to explore state management solutions like **Redux** or **MobX**.

In the next chapter, we will explore **Redux** and its integration with React for more advanced state management in large applications.

CHAPTER 12

OPTIMIZING PERFORMANCE IN REACT

Performance Issues in React and How to Avoid Them

React is designed to be efficient, but as applications grow in size and complexity, performance can become an issue. React's re-rendering process is one of the key areas that can affect performance. The primary challenge in React is managing re-renders to avoid unnecessary updates that can degrade the performance of your app.

Common Performance Issues in React:

1. **Excessive Re-renders**: React re-renders components when their state or props change. If a component's state or props change frequently, it may trigger re-renders that are not necessary, which can slow down your app.

2. **Unoptimized Lists**: Rendering large lists or tables of data without optimizing can lead to performance issues. For example, rendering a list of hundreds or thousands of items in a single go can cause slow rendering and poor user experience.

3. **Expensive Calculations**: If you have components that perform heavy computations or calculations, they may slow down the entire app, especially when re-rendered frequently.

4. **Large Bundle Size**: If your app contains many dependencies or large libraries, it can increase the initial load time, affecting the user experience.

How to Optimize Performance:

- **Minimize unnecessary re-renders**: Ensure components only re-render when necessary.

- **Optimize list rendering**: Use techniques like **virtualization** to render only the visible items in large lists.

- **Lazy load components**: Load components only when they are needed, reducing the initial load time.

- **Memoization**: Avoid recalculating expensive operations or re-rendering components unnecessarily by memoizing them.

Lazy Loading Components with React.lazy() and Suspense

Lazy loading is a technique where components are loaded only when they are needed, rather than all at once during the initial load. This helps reduce the initial bundle size and improves the app's loading time.

React provides a built-in function `React.lazy()` for lazy loading components, and `Suspense` to handle the loading state while the component is being fetched.

How `React.lazy()` and `Suspense` Work:

1. `React.lazy()` is used to dynamically import a component.
2. `Suspense` is used to specify a fallback UI (e.g., a loading spinner) while the component is being loaded.

Example of Lazy Loading a Component:

```javascript
import React, { Suspense } from 'react';

// Lazy load the ProductDetails component
const ProductDetails = React.lazy(() =>
import('./ProductDetails'));

function ProductPage() {
  return (
    <div>
      <h1>Product Page</h1>
```

```
    <Suspense
fallback={<div>Loading...</div>}>
        <ProductDetails />
      </Suspense>
    </div>
  );
}
```

```
export default ProductPage;
```

In this example:

- `ProductDetails` is lazily loaded using `React.lazy()`.
- While `ProductDetails` is being loaded, the fallback `<div>Loading...</div>` is shown.
- Once the component is loaded, it will be rendered normally.

Why Use Lazy Loading:

- **Faster initial load**: Only load the components that are needed initially, reducing the app's initial bundle size.
- **Improved performance**: Load components dynamically as the user navigates through the app, which helps in reducing the load time.

Memoization Techniques with React.memo() and useMemo()

Memoization is an optimization technique that helps avoid recalculating values or re-rendering components unnecessarily by caching the result of expensive operations.

1. React.memo():

`React.memo()` is a higher-order component (HOC) that wraps a functional component and prevents it from re-rendering if its props haven't changed.

It's particularly useful for **functional components** that receive the same props over time and don't need to re-render on each state change.

Example of React.memo():

javascript

```
const Product = React.memo(function Product({
name, price }) {
  console.log('Rendering product:', name);
  return (
    <div>
      <h2>{name}</h2>
      <p>{price}</p>
    </div>
  );
```

```
});

function ProductList({ products }) {
  return (
    <div>
      {products.map((product) => (
        <Product                key={product.id}
name={product.name} price={product.price} />
      ))}
    </div>
  );
}
```

In this example:

- The `Product` component will only re-render if the `name` or `price` props change.
- If the parent component (`ProductList`) re-renders with the same product data, `Product` will not re-render, improving performance.

2. useMemo():

The `useMemo()` hook is used to memoize expensive calculations or values that are derived from props or state. It ensures that the calculation is only recomputed when the dependencies change, rather than on every render.

Example of useMemo():

```javascript

import React, { useMemo } from 'react';

function ProductList({ products, filter }) {
  const filteredProducts = useMemo(() => {
    return     products.filter((product)      =>
product.name.includes(filter));
  }, [filter, products]); // Recalculate only
when filter or products change

  return (
    <div>
      {filteredProducts.map((product) => (
        <div
key={product.id}>{product.name}</div>
      ))}
    </div>
  );
}
```

In this example:

- useMemo() ensures that the filtered list of products is only recalculated when filter or products change.
- If neither filter nor products changes, the memoized result is returned, avoiding unnecessary re-calculation.

Why Use Memoization:

- **Avoid unnecessary re-renders**: Components or calculations that depend on the same data should not be recomputed every time the component re-renders.
- **Improve performance**: Memoization can significantly improve performance in large applications with complex UI updates and data transformations.

Example: Improving Performance in a Product Listing Page

Let's apply the performance optimization techniques (lazy loading, memoization) to a **Product Listing Page** that dynamically fetches product data, lazily loads product details, and optimizes re-renders using `React.memo()`.

1. Lazy Load Product Details:

We will use `React.lazy()` and `Suspense` to lazy-load product detail components when needed.

javascript

```
import React, { useState, useEffect, Suspense }
from 'react';

// Lazy load ProductDetails component
```

```
const    ProductDetails    =    React.lazy(()    =>
import('./ProductDetails'));

function ProductPage() {
  const [products, setProducts] = useState([]);

  useEffect(() => {
    fetch('/api/products')
      .then((response) => response.json())
      .then((data) => setProducts(data));
  }, []);

  return (
    <div>
      <h1>Product Listing</h1>
      <Suspense  fallback={<div>Loading  product
details...</div>}>
        {products.map((product) => (
        <ProductDetails       key={product.id}
product={product} />
        ))}
      </Suspense>
    </div>
  );
}

export default ProductPage;
```

2. Memoize Product List Rendering:

We will use `React.memo()` to optimize re-renders of the `Product` component.

javascript

```javascript
const Product = React.memo(({ name, price }) =>
{
  console.log('Rendering product:', name);
  return (
    <div>
      <h2>{name}</h2>
      <p>{price}</p>
    </div>
  );
});

function ProductList({ products }) {
  return (
    <div>
      {products.map((product) => (
        <Product                  key={product.id}
name={product.name} price={product.price} />
      ))}
    </div>
  );
}
```

3. Memoize Expensive Calculations:

We will use `useMemo()` to avoid recalculating the filtered list of products unnecessarily.

```javascript
import React, { useMemo } from 'react';

function ProductList({ products, filter }) {
  const filteredProducts = useMemo(() => {
    return     products.filter((product)     =>
product.name.includes(filter));
  }, [filter, products]); // Recalculate only
when filter or products change

  return (
    <div>
      {filteredProducts.map((product) => (
        <div
key={product.id}>{product.name}</div>
      ))}
    </div>
  );
}
```

Conclusion

In this chapter, we learned how to **optimize performance** in React applications by:

- Using **lazy loading** with `React.lazy()` and `Suspense` to defer loading components until they are needed.
- Applying **memoization** techniques like `React.memo()` and `useMemo()` to avoid unnecessary re-renders and expensive calculations.
- We demonstrated these techniques in a **Product Listing Page**, showing how to improve performance in a dynamic, data-driven application.

These optimizations are essential for building fast, responsive React apps, especially as they grow in size and complexity. In the next chapter, we will explore more advanced performance techniques, such as **code splitting** and **virtualization** for large datasets.

CHAPTER 13

STYLING REACT COMPONENTS

Approaches to Styling in React

There are several ways to apply styles in React applications, each with its own benefits and trade-offs. The three most commonly used approaches for styling React components are **inline styles, CSS modules**, and **styled-components**.

1. Inline Styles

Inline styles in React are simply JavaScript objects that define the CSS properties for an element. These styles are applied directly to a component's JSX elements using the `style` attribute.

Pros:

- Quick and easy to implement.
- Styles are scoped to the specific element.

Cons:

- Limited to simple styles (e.g., dynamic styles like hover states or media queries are not easy to implement).
- Styles are not reusable.

Example of Inline Styles:

```javascript
import React from 'react';

function Button() {
  const buttonStyle = {
    backgroundColor: 'blue',
    color: 'white',
    padding: '10px 20px',
    borderRadius: '5px',
    cursor: 'pointer',
  };

  return <button style={buttonStyle}>Click Me</button>;
}

export default Button;
```

In this example:

- We define a `buttonStyle` object containing CSS properties.
- The `style` attribute is applied directly to the `<button>` element.

2. CSS Modules

CSS Modules provide a way to locally scope CSS styles, ensuring that styles are applied only to the component they are imported into. This is done by generating unique class names for each component, preventing class name collisions.

Pros:

- Styles are scoped locally to the component, preventing global CSS conflicts.
- Supports full CSS features (e.g., hover states, media queries, etc.).

Cons:

- Requires additional build setup (e.g., Webpack) for React projects.
- Cannot use inline styles or JavaScript objects directly for styles.

Example of CSS Modules:

1. **Create a CSS file (e.g., `Button.module.css`)**:

css

```
/* Button.module.css */
.button {
```

145

```css
background-color: blue;
color: white;
padding: 10px 20px;
border-radius: 5px;
cursor: pointer;
}


.button:hover {
background-color: darkblue;
}
```

2. Use CSS module in a React component:

```
javascript
```

```javascript
import React from 'react';
import styles from './Button.module.css';

function Button() {
  return <button className={styles.button}>Click
Me</button>;
}


export default Button;
```

In this example:

- The `Button.module.css` file contains the CSS styles for the `Button` component.

- We import the styles and apply them using `className={styles.button}`, which ensures that the styles are scoped to the component.

3. Styled-Components

Styled-components is a popular library for styling React components using tagged template literals. It allows you to write actual CSS syntax inside your JavaScript files, and it automatically handles scoped styles for you. Styled-components are **dynamic** and support theming, nesting, and more advanced features like media queries.

Pros:

- Styles are scoped automatically.
- Fully supports dynamic styles and theming.
- Supports all CSS features, including nesting, media queries, and animations.
- Promotes component-based design by styling each component individually.

Cons:

- Adds an extra dependency to your project.
- Can increase bundle size if not used efficiently.

Example of Styled-Components:

bash

npm install styled-components

1. **Creating a styled component**:

javascript

```javascript
import React from 'react';
import styled from 'styled-components';

// Define a styled button
const Button = styled.button`
  background-color: blue;
  color: white;
  padding: 10px 20px;
  border-radius: 5px;
  cursor: pointer;

  &:hover {
    background-color: darkblue;
  }
`;

function App() {
  return <Button>Click Me</Button>;
}

export default App;
```

In this example:

- The `Button` component is styled using `styled.button` from the `styled-components` library.
- We use template literals to define the CSS for the button directly in the JavaScript file.

Using Styled-Components for Dynamic Theming

One of the most powerful features of **styled-components** is the ability to create dynamic themes that can change at runtime. This is achieved using **props** and **theme providers**.

1. Creating a Theme Provider:

You can define a **theme** that contains all the colors, fonts, and other styling variables for your app. Then, use the `ThemeProvider` component from styled-components to apply the theme globally.

Example: Dynamic Theming with Styled-Components:

```javascript
import React, { useState } from 'react';
import styled, { ThemeProvider } from 'styled-components';
```

```
// Define the light and dark themes
const lightTheme = {
  background: '#ffffff',
  color: '#000000',
};

const darkTheme = {
  background: '#333333',
  color: '#ffffff',
};

// Create a styled component
const Container = styled.div`
  background-color:        ${(props)        =>
props.theme.background};
  color: ${(props) => props.theme.color};
  padding: 20px;
  text-align: center;
`;

const Button = styled.button`
  background-color:        ${(props)        =>
props.theme.color};
  color: ${(props) => props.theme.background};
  padding: 10px;
  border: none;
  cursor: pointer;
`;
```

```
function App() {
  const [isDark, setIsDark] = useState(false);

  const toggleTheme = () => {
    setIsDark((prev) => !prev);
  };

  return (
    <ThemeProvider theme={isDark ? darkTheme :
lightTheme}>
      <Container>
        <h1>React    Theming    with    Styled-
Components</h1>
        <Button onClick={toggleTheme}>
          Switch to {isDark ? 'Light' : 'Dark'}
Theme
        </Button>
      </Container>
    </ThemeProvider>
  );
}


export default App;
```

In this example:

- We define two themes: lightTheme and darkTheme.

- The `Container` and `Button` styled components use values from the current theme (via `props.theme`).

- The `ThemeProvider` component from styled-components wraps the app, making the selected theme available to all styled components inside it.

- A button toggles between the light and dark themes when clicked.

Why Use Styled-Components for Theming:

- **Dynamic Styles**: You can easily apply different styles based on props, enabling you to create a dynamic and interactive UI.

- **Global Theme Management**: The `ThemeProvider` allows you to manage global styles in one place, making it easy to change themes across your app.

- **Scoped Styles**: Each styled component has its styles scoped automatically, preventing style conflicts and improving maintainability.

Example: Creating a Responsive Card Component with Styled-Components

Now, let's create a **responsive card component** using styled-components. The card will adjust its layout based on screen size using media queries.

152

```javascript

import React from 'react';
import styled from 'styled-components';

// Create a styled card component with responsive
styles
const Card = styled.div`
  background-color: #fff;
  border-radius: 8px;
  box-shadow: 0 4px 8px rgba(0, 0, 0, 0.1);
  overflow: hidden;
  width: 300px;
  margin: 20px;
  transition: all 0.3s ease;

  &:hover {
    box-shadow: 0 6px 12px rgba(0, 0, 0, 0.2);
  }

  @media (max-width: 768px) {
    width: 100%;
  }
`;

const CardHeader = styled.div`
  background-color: #f8f8f8;
  padding: 20px;
  font-size: 18px;
```

```
    font-weight: bold;
`;


const CardBody = styled.div`
  padding: 20px;
  font-size: 16px;
  color: #333;
`;


function CardComponent() {
  return (
    <Card>
      <CardHeader>Responsive Card</CardHeader>
      <CardBody>
        This card adjusts its size based on the
screen width. Resize the window to
        see the effect.
      </CardBody>
    </Card>
  );
}


export default CardComponent;
```

In this example:

- The Card component has a width of 300px by default but changes to 100% width when the screen size is less than 768px, making it responsive.

- The `CardHeader` and `CardBody` components are used to structure the card content.

Responsive Design:

- We use **media queries** within the `styled-components` to make the card responsive to different screen sizes.
- The hover effect on the card adds a smooth transition for better interactivity.

Conclusion

In this chapter, we explored various **approaches to styling in React**:

- **Inline styles** for quick styling but limited in functionality.
- **CSS modules** for locally scoped styles, reducing the chance of style conflicts.
- **Styled-components**, which allow for component-level styling, dynamic theming, and responsive design using media queries.

We also explored how to create **dynamic theming** with **styled-components** and how to create a **responsive card component** that adjusts based on the screen size. These techniques are essential for building modern, maintainable, and scalable React applications.

155

In the next chapter, we will dive into **form handling** and **validation**, including how to manage form input, validate user input, and provide feedback to users.

CHAPTER 14

INTRODUCTION TO FULL-STACK DEVELOPMENT WITH REACT

Overview of Full-Stack Development

Full-stack development refers to the development of both the front-end (client-side) and back-end (server-side) of a web application. It involves working with both the **UI** that users interact with (the front-end) and the **server** that handles business logic, databases, and data communication (the back-end). Full-stack developers have knowledge of both front-end and back-end technologies and can build complete applications from start to finish.

A **full-stack application** typically consists of:

1. **Front-end**: The part of the application that interacts directly with the user. It is responsible for rendering the UI, handling user interactions, and displaying data. React is one of the most popular libraries for building the front-end.

2. **Back-end**: The server-side part of the application that processes requests, manages data, and communicates with

databases. The back-end can be built using various technologies like Node.js, Python, Ruby, or Java.

3. **Database**: This stores and retrieves data for the application. Common databases include MongoDB, PostgreSQL, and MySQL.

Full-stack developers need to understand how the front-end communicates with the back-end, and how the back-end interacts with the database. This chapter will focus on the role of **React** in front-end development and how to set up a simple back-end using **Node.js** and **Express**.

The Role of React in Front-End Development and Interacting with Back-End APIs

React plays a crucial role in front-end development by allowing developers to build dynamic user interfaces. It focuses on creating reusable components, managing state, and efficiently updating the UI in response to changes in data.

In full-stack development, React is typically responsible for rendering the UI and interacting with the back-end to fetch and send data. This is done through **APIs (Application Programming Interfaces)**, which allow the front-end to communicate with the back-end.

React's Role:

- **Building UI**: React is used to build the UI by creating components that manage their own state and render content dynamically.
- **Fetching Data**: React communicates with the back-end using APIs (usually RESTful APIs or GraphQL) to fetch data and display it on the UI.
- **Handling User Interaction**: React listens for user events (like clicks, form submissions) and sends requests to the back-end for processing.

React does not handle the back-end logic directly; instead, it interacts with back-end APIs to request or send data, and the back-end processes these requests, interacting with the database when necessary.

Setting Up a Simple Back-End with Node.js and Express

Node.js is a JavaScript runtime that allows you to run JavaScript code outside of the browser, typically on the server. **Express** is a lightweight web application framework built on top of Node.js, providing a robust set of tools for building back-end applications.

To build a full-stack application with React, we need to set up the back-end with Node.js and Express, create routes to handle requests, and use these routes to interact with the front-end.

Steps to Set Up a Simple Back-End with Node.js and Express:

1. **Install Node.js**: Make sure you have Node.js installed on your machine. You can download it from nodejs.org.

2. **Initialize the Back-End Project**:
   - In your project directory, run the following command to initialize a Node.js project:

   ```bash
   npm init -y
   ```

   - This creates a `package.json` file where you can list your project dependencies.

3. **Install Express**:
   - Install Express using the following command:

   ```bash
   npm install express
   ```

4. **Create the Server**:
   - Create a file named `server.js` to define your back-end server.

   ```javascript
   const express = require('express');
   const app = express();
   ```

160

```
const port = 5000;

// Middleware to parse JSON requests
app.use(express.json());

// Sample route to send a response
app.get('/', (req, res) => {
  res.send('Hello      from      the
server!');
});

// Start the server
app.listen(port, () => {
  console.log(`Server    running    on
http://localhost:${port}`);
});
```

- In this example:
  - We import the express library and create an Express app.
  - We set up a route that responds to a GET request at / with a message: "Hello from the server!".
  - The app listens on port 5000.

5. **Run the Server**:
   - To start the server, run the following command in the terminal:

   ```bash
   bash
   ```

```
node server.js
```

- o This will start the back-end server on `http://localhost:5000`.

Example: Building a Simple Full-Stack App with React and Node.js

Now that we have set up a simple back-end with Node.js and Express, let's create a **full-stack app** where the React front-end communicates with the Node.js back-end.

1. Set Up the Front-End (React App):

1. **Create the React App**:
   - o In a separate directory, create a React app using `create-react-app`:

     bash

     ```
     npx create-react-app react-client
     ```

2. **Fetch Data from the Back-End**:
   - o In the React app, you can use the `useEffect` hook to fetch data from the back-end when the component mounts. For this example, we will fetch a simple message from the server.

162

In `src/App.js`, update the code as follows:

javascript

```javascript
import React, { useState, useEffect } from 'react';

function App() {
  const [message, setMessage] = useState('');

  // Fetch data from the back-end server
  useEffect(() => {
    fetch('http://localhost:5000')
      .then((response) => response.text())
      .then((data) => setMessage(data));
  }, []);

  return (
    <div>
      <h1>Full-Stack App</h1>
      <p>{message}</p>
    </div>
  );
}

export default App;
```

- o In this example:
  - We use the `useEffect` hook to fetch data from the back-end when the component mounts.
  - The data (a simple message) returned from the server is set in the `message` state and displayed in the UI.

3. **Run the React App**:
   - o In the React app's directory (`react-client`), start the development server:

   bash

   ```
   npm start
   ```

   - o The React app will run on `http://localhost:3000`.

2. Set Up CORS (Cross-Origin Resource Sharing):

When your front-end and back-end are running on different ports (React on `3000` and Node.js on `5000`), you need to enable **CORS** (Cross-Origin Resource Sharing) to allow communication between them.

1. **Install CORS in Node.js**:
   - o Install the `cors` package in your Node.js back-end:

```
bash
```

```
npm install cors
```

2. **Enable CORS in the Back-End**:

- o In `server.js`, add the following lines to enable CORS:

```javascript
const cors = require('cors');
app.use(cors());
```

- o This allows your React app to make requests to the back-end without running into security issues related to different origins.

3. Testing the Full-Stack App:

Now that both the front-end and back-end are set up, go to `http://localhost:3000` in your browser. You should see the React app displaying the message fetched from the Node.js back-end.

Conclusion

In this chapter, we explored **full-stack development** with React, focusing on how React interacts with a back-end API built using Node.js and Express. We:

- Set up a simple Node.js and Express server.
- Built a React front-end that communicates with the back-end API.
- Used **CORS** to enable cross-origin requests.
- Created a **full-stack app** where React fetches data from the back-end and displays it on the front-end.

By combining React's front-end capabilities with Node.js and Express for back-end logic, you can build powerful full-stack applications. In the next chapter, we will explore **authentication and authorization** in full-stack apps, including how to implement secure login systems using JSON Web Tokens (JWT).

CHAPTER 15

DATA FETCHING WITH REACT

Introduction to `fetch()` *and* `axios` *for Making HTTP Requests*

In modern web applications, interacting with external APIs to retrieve or send data is a fundamental task. React does not provide a built-in solution for making HTTP requests, but there are two popular methods for handling data fetching in React:

1. **fetch()**:

    o `fetch()` is a built-in JavaScript function for making HTTP requests. It returns a **Promise** that resolves to the `Response` object, which represents the response to the request.

    o It is widely supported in modern browsers and is relatively simple to use, but it requires manual handling of response parsing and error handling.

Example:

```javascript
fetch('https://api.example.com/data')
```

```
.then(response => response.json())    //
Parse the response as JSON
   .then(data => console.log(data))      //
Use the fetched data
   .catch(error => console.error('Error:',
error));   // Handle errors
```

2. **axios**:

   o   `axios` is a popular third-party library for making HTTP requests. It is promise-based and provides a cleaner, more user-friendly API than `fetch()`. It handles JSON parsing and error handling automatically.

   o   Axios supports older browsers and has additional features such as request/response interceptors, request cancellation, and automatic JSON parsing.

Example:

javascript

```
import axios from 'axios';

axios.get('https://api.example.com/data')
   .then(response                        =>
console.log(response.data))    // Data  is
automatically parsed
```

```
.catch(error => console.error('Error:',
error));  // Handle errors
```

In this chapter, we will use both `fetch()` and `axios` to demonstrate how data fetching works in React.

Handling Asynchronous Data Fetching with React Hooks

In React, **data fetching** often involves asynchronous operations, which means that we need to handle asynchronous behavior effectively. This is usually done by using **React Hooks**, specifically the `useEffect` hook, which allows you to perform side effects such as data fetching after the component has rendered.

The general process of fetching data in React involves:

1. **Setting the state** for the data once the request is complete.
2. **Handling loading state** to show the user that the data is being fetched.
3. **Handling errors** to catch issues with the request.

We will use the `useState` and `useEffect` hooks to fetch and display data in a functional React component.

Steps for Handling Asynchronous Data Fetching:

1. Use the `useState` hook to manage the state of the fetched data and loading/error states.
2. Use the `useEffect` hook to trigger the data fetching when the component mounts.
3. Display the data, loading state, and error messages accordingly.

Example: Fetching and Displaying Weather Data from an External API

In this example, we will create a **weather app** that fetches data from a public weather API and displays it. We will use the **OpenWeatherMap API** (https://openweathermap.org/api) for this example. You will need an API key, but for demonstration purposes, we will use a generic endpoint.

1. Setting Up the Weather Component

First, install `axios` if you prefer using it instead of `fetch()`:

bash

```
npm install axios
```

Now, let's build a simple **weather fetching component**.

```javascript

import React, { useState, useEffect } from
'react';
import axios from 'axios';

function WeatherApp() {
  const [weatherData, setWeatherData] =
useState(null);
  const [loading, setLoading] = useState(true);
  const [error, setError] = useState(null);
  const [city, setCity] = useState('London');  //
Default city is London

  useEffect(() => {
    const fetchWeatherData = async () => {
      try {
        setLoading(true);
        const response = await axios.get(

`https://api.openweathermap.org/data/2.5/weathe
r?q=${city}&appid=YOUR_API_KEY`
        );
        setWeatherData(response.data);
        setLoading(false);
      } catch (error) {
        setError('Failed to fetch weather
data');
        setLoading(false);
```

```
      }
    };


    fetchWeatherData();
  }, [city]); // Re-fetch data whenever the city
changes

  const handleCityChange = (event) => {
    setCity(event.target.value);
  };

  if (loading) {
    return <div>Loading weather data...</div>;
  }

  if (error) {
    return <div>{error}</div>;
  }

  return (
    <div>
      <h1>Weather in {weatherData.name}</h1>
      <h2>{Math.round(weatherData.main.temp    -
273.15)}°C</h2>

<p>{weatherData.weather[0].description}</p>

      <input
        type="text"
```

```
      value={city}
      onChange={handleCityChange}
      placeholder="Enter city name"
    />
  </div>
);
}
```

```
export default WeatherApp;
```

Explanation of the Code:

1. **State Management**:

   o `weatherData`: Stores the weather data fetched from the API.

   o `loading`: Tracks the loading state while waiting for the data to be fetched.

   o `error`: Stores any error messages encountered during the data fetching.

   o `city`: Stores the current city name entered by the user.

2. **useEffect**:

   o The `useEffect` hook runs the `fetchWeatherData` function when the component is first mounted and whenever the `city` changes.

- o We use `axios` to send a GET request to the OpenWeatherMap API and fetch the weather data for the specified city.

3. **Error Handling**:
   - o If there is an error (e.g., invalid city name or network issues), the error message is displayed.

4. **City Input**:
   - o We provide an input field to allow the user to change the city. When the city is changed, the weather data is re-fetched.

5. **Displaying Data**:
   - o Once the data is successfully fetched, we display the city name, temperature (converted from Kelvin to Celsius), and weather description.

Using `fetch()` for Data Fetching (Alternative)

Instead of using `axios`, you can use the native `fetch()` API to retrieve the weather data. Here's how you can rewrite the `fetchWeatherData` function using `fetch()`:

javascript

```javascript
const fetchWeatherData = async () => {
  try {
    setLoading(true);
    const response = await fetch(
```

```
`https://api.openweathermap.org/data/2.5/weathe
r?q=${city}&appid=YOUR_API_KEY`
    );
    const data = await response.json();
    setWeatherData(data);
    setLoading(false);
  } catch (error) {
    setError('Failed to fetch weather data');
    setLoading(false);
  }
};
```

The rest of the logic stays the same as with `axios`, but `fetch()` requires you to manually parse the JSON response using `.json()`.

Handling Asynchronous Data Fetching and State Updates

When dealing with asynchronous operations like data fetching, there are several important things to consider:

1. **Loading State**: Always show a loading indicator (e.g., "Loading...") while the data is being fetched to improve the user experience.
2. **Error Handling**: Ensure that any errors encountered during data fetching (e.g., network errors, invalid

responses) are caught and handled properly. This allows you to display an appropriate error message to the user.

3. **Conditional Rendering**: You can use conditional rendering to show different UI elements depending on the state of the data (e.g., show a loading message while fetching, show the weather once it's fetched).

Conclusion

In this chapter, we covered **data fetching** in React using two popular methods: `fetch()` and `axios`. We:

- Discussed how to use `fetch()` and `axios` to make HTTP requests and handle asynchronous operations.
- Used the **useState** and **useEffect** hooks to manage the loading, error, and data states in React components.
- Built a **weather app** that fetches weather data from an external API and displays it, with error handling and user input for dynamic city searches.

Data fetching is an essential part of modern web development, and React provides a straightforward way to manage asynchronous data using hooks. In the next chapter, we will explore **state management** and how to use tools like the **Context API** and **Redux** for managing global state across components.

CHAPTER 16

AUTHENTICATION AND AUTHORIZATION IN REACT

Understanding Authentication in Modern Web Apps

Authentication and **authorization** are two fundamental concepts in modern web development that are essential for securing user data and controlling access to different parts of an application.

- **Authentication**: This is the process of verifying a user's identity. In web applications, this typically involves verifying a user's username and password, or using third-party authentication providers like Google or Facebook.

- **Authorization**: Once a user is authenticated, authorization determines what actions the user can perform or what data they can access. This ensures that users only have access to the resources they are allowed to.

Modern web applications often rely on **JSON Web Tokens (JWT)** for both authentication and authorization. JWTs are a compact, URL-safe means of representing claims between two parties (usually between a client and a server).

Setting Up JWT-Based Authentication in React

JSON Web Tokens (JWT) are widely used for authentication because they are stateless and can be stored on the client side, typically in **localStorage** or **sessionStorage**.

How JWT-Based Authentication Works:

1. **User Login**: The user submits their credentials (e.g., username and password) to the server.
2. **Server Validation**: The server validates the credentials and, if they are correct, generates a JWT.
3. **Token Storage**: The JWT is sent back to the client, where it is stored (usually in localStorage or sessionStorage).
4. **Token Usage**: The client includes the JWT in the headers of subsequent API requests to prove their identity and gain access to protected routes or data.
5. **Token Expiration**: The JWT has an expiration date, and once expired, the user needs to re-authenticate.

Setting Up JWT Authentication Flow:

Here is an outline of the steps involved in setting up JWT-based authentication in a React application:

1. **Set Up the Back-End (Node.js & Express)**:
   o Create an API endpoint for login that validates user credentials and returns a JWT.

2. **Set Up the Front-End (React)**:

    o   Create a login form.

    o   Handle form submission to send credentials to the back-end API.

    o   Store the JWT in the browser (localStorage or sessionStorage).

    o   Attach the JWT to the `Authorization` header in API requests to protected routes.

Real-World Example: Implementing a Login System in a React App

Let's walk through how to implement a simple login system in a React app using JWT-based authentication.

1. Back-End Setup (Node.js & Express)

First, let's set up the back-end to handle authentication and generate JWTs.

1. **Install Dependencies**:

    o   Install Express, JWT, bcrypt (for password hashing), and other necessary packages.

    bash

    ```
    npm install express jsonwebtoken bcryptjs
    dotenv
    ```

2. Create the Login Route:

javascript

```javascript
const express = require('express');
const jwt = require('jsonwebtoken');
const bcrypt = require('bcryptjs');
const app = express();
const port = 5000;

// Middleware to parse JSON
app.use(express.json());

// Sample user data (in a real app, this should
be in a database)
const users = [
  { id: 1, username: 'user1', password:
'$2a$10$uOQ8IbmRgH/v4XDRHK2qOupbQlVTHrrjrHgD/O5
dve8kRYWWlHe3C' }, // password: "password"
];

// Login route
app.post('/login', (req, res) => {
  const { username, password } = req.body;

  // Check if the user exists
  const user = users.find((u) => u.username ===
username);
  if (!user) {
```

```
    return res.status(400).json({ message: 'User
not found' });
  }

  // Check if password is correct
  bcrypt.compare(password, user.password, (err,
isMatch) => {
    if (err) throw err;
    if (!isMatch) {
      return   res.status(400).json({   message:
'Invalid credentials' });
    }

    // Create JWT token
    const   token   =   jwt.sign({   id:   user.id,
username:   user.username   },   'secretkey',   {
expiresIn: '1h' });

    // Send the token to the client
    res.json({ token });
  });
});

app.listen(port,   ()   =>   console.log(`Server
running on http://localhost:${port}`));
```

In this back-end code:

- We create a simple Express server with a /login route.

181

- The server checks if the provided username exists and if the password matches using bcrypt.
- If authentication is successful, a JWT is generated and sent to the client.

---

2. Front-End Setup (React)

Now, let's implement the login functionality in React.

1. **Create the Login Form**:

javascript

```javascript
import React, { useState } from 'react';

function Login() {
  const [username, setUsername] = useState('');
  const [password, setPassword] = useState('');
  const [error, setError] = useState('');
  const [loading, setLoading] = useState(false);

  const handleLogin = async (event) => {
    event.preventDefault();
    setLoading(true);
    setError('');

    try {
```

```
    const        response       =        await
fetch('http://localhost:5000/login', {
      method: 'POST',
      headers: {
        'Content-Type': 'application/json',
      },
      body:      JSON.stringify({      username,
password }),
    });

    const data = await response.json();
    if (response.ok) {
      // Save the token to localStorage
      localStorage.setItem('token',
data.token);
      setLoading(false);
      alert('Login successful');
    } else {
      setError(data.message);
      setLoading(false);
    }
  } catch (error) {
    setError('Something went wrong');
    setLoading(false);
  }
};

return (
  <div>
```

```jsx
<h1>Login</h1>
<form onSubmit={handleLogin}>
  <div>
    <label>Username</label>
    <input
      type="text"
      value={username}
      onChange={(e)                        =>
setUsername(e.target.value)}
      required
    />
  </div>
  <div>
    <label>Password</label>
    <input
      type="password"
      value={password}
      onChange={(e)                        =>
setPassword(e.target.value)}
      required
    />
  </div>
  {error && <div style={{ color: 'red'
}}>{error}</div>}
  <button                        type="submit"
disabled={loading}>
    {loading ? 'Logging in...' : 'Login'}
  </button>
</form>
```

```
    </div>
  );
}
```

```
export default Login;
```

In this front-end code:

- We create a simple login form that captures the `username` and `password` values.
- When the user submits the form, the `handleLogin` function sends a POST request to the `/login` route in the back-end with the user credentials.
- If the login is successful, the JWT token is stored in `localStorage` for future requests.
- We handle loading and error states to provide feedback to the user.

3. Protecting Routes with JWT

To protect certain routes in your React app, you can check if a valid JWT is stored in `localStorage` and include it in the `Authorization` header when making API requests.

Example of a protected API request:

```
javascript
```

```
const fetchUserData = async () => {
  const token = localStorage.getItem('token');
  const          response          =          await
fetch('http://localhost:5000/protected', {
    method: 'GET',
    headers: {
      'Authorization': `Bearer ${token}`,
    },
  });

  const data = await response.json();
  console.log(data);
};
```

Conclusion

In this chapter, we explored the concepts of **authentication** and **authorization** in React applications, focusing on JWT-based authentication. We:

- Set up a **back-end** with **Node.js** and **Express** to handle login and generate JWTs.
- Built a **React front-end** to handle login, store JWTs in localStorage, and send them with API requests.
- Discussed how to protect routes and require authentication for accessing certain parts of the app.

JWT-based authentication is widely used in modern web apps because it's stateless, secure, and easy to implement. In the next chapter, we will dive deeper into **authorization**, including role-based access control and permissions, for more advanced security mechanisms in your applications.

CHAPTER 17

MANAGING COMPLEX STATE WITH REDUX

Introduction to Redux and Why It's Useful for Managing Complex State

In modern React applications, managing state can become complicated as the app grows in size. When multiple components need to access or modify shared state, managing that state with **React's built-in state management** (via `useState` or `useReducer`) can become cumbersome. This is where **Redux** comes in.

Redux is a predictable state container for JavaScript apps. It allows you to manage the application state in a central **store** and provides a strict unidirectional data flow, making state changes easier to reason about and debug. Redux is often used in larger applications where managing state across many components can become complex and difficult to maintain.

Why Use Redux?

1. **Centralized State Management**: With Redux, all the application state is stored in a single place, called the **store**, making it easy to access and update the state from any component.

2. **Predictable State**: Redux uses **actions** and **reducers** to modify the state in a predictable way. Actions are dispatched to trigger state changes, and reducers update the state based on the action type.

3. **Easier Debugging**: Since Redux follows a predictable flow, you can easily track actions and state changes, which helps in debugging and understanding how the state evolves.

4. **Decoupling of Components**: Components do not need to pass props down multiple layers. They can access the state from the Redux store, making component communication simpler.

Setting Up Redux with React

To use Redux with React, we need to install the necessary libraries and set up a store that will hold the state of our application.

Step 1: Install Redux and React-Redux

1. First, install `redux` and `react-redux` (the official Redux bindings for React).

bash

```
npm install redux react-redux
```

- `redux`: This is the core Redux library that provides tools to manage the state.
- `react-redux`: This library connects React components to the Redux store.

Step 2: Create the Redux Store

The Redux store holds the entire application's state. You will typically use a **reducer** to define how the state is updated based on actions dispatched to the store.

1. **Create a Reducer**: A reducer is a function that takes the current state and an action as arguments, then returns a new state.

javascript

```
// reducer.js
const initialState = {
  count: 0
```

```
};

function   counterReducer(state   =   initialState,
action) {
  switch (action.type) {
    case 'INCREMENT':
      return { count: state.count + 1 };
    case 'DECREMENT':
      return { count: state.count - 1 };
    default:
      return state;
  }
}

export default counterReducer;
```

- In this example, the reducer manages a count state and handles two actions: INCREMENT and DECREMENT.

2. **Create the Store**: The Redux store combines the reducers and holds the application state.

```
javascript
```

```javascript
// store.js
import { createStore } from 'redux';
import counterReducer from './reducer';

// Create the Redux store with the reducer
```

```
const store = createStore(counterReducer);

export default store;
```

- `createStore` is used to create the Redux store and pass in the reducer.

Step 3: Connect Redux Store to React

To allow React components to interact with the Redux store, you need to use the `Provider` component from `react-redux` to wrap your application.

javascript

```
// index.js
import React from 'react';
import ReactDOM from 'react-dom';
import { Provider } from 'react-redux';
import App from './App';
import store from './store';

// Wrap the App with the Provider component and
pass in the Redux store
ReactDOM.render(
  <Provider store={store}>
    <App />
  </Provider>,
  document.getElementById('root')
```

```
);
```

- The `Provider` component makes the Redux store available to all components in the application.

Actions, Reducers, and the Store

Now that we've set up Redux in our React app, let's dive into the core concepts of **actions**, **reducers**, and the **store**.

1. **Actions**:
   - o Actions are plain JavaScript objects that describe what happened. They must have a `type` property, which is a string that indicates the action's type.
   - o Actions may also contain additional data (payload) that the reducer uses to update the state.

javascript

```javascript
// actions.js
export const increment = () => {
  return {
    type: 'INCREMENT'
  };
};

export const decrement = () => {
  return {
```

```
    type: 'DECREMENT'
  };
};
```

- In this example, `increment` and `decrement` are action creators that return action objects with a `type` property.

2. **Reducers**:
  - ○ Reducers are pure functions that take the current state and an action as input and return a new state.
  - ○ Each reducer handles a specific type of action and updates the state accordingly.

```javascript
// reducer.js
const initialState = {
  count: 0
};

function counterReducer(state = initialState,
action) {
  switch (action.type) {
    case 'INCREMENT':
      return { count: state.count + 1 };
    case 'DECREMENT':
      return { count: state.count - 1 };
    default:
      return state;
```

194

```
    }
}
```

3. **Store**:
   - The store holds the entire application state. It is created using the `createStore` function from the Redux library.
   - The store is passed to the `Provider` component so that all React components can access the state.

javascript

```
// store.js
import { createStore } from 'redux';
import counterReducer from './reducer';

// Create Redux store
const store = createStore(counterReducer);

export default store;
```

Real-World Example: Building a Shopping Cart App with Redux

Let's build a simple **shopping cart** app where we will manage the cart's state (items, total price, etc.) using Redux.

Step 1: Set Up the Redux Store

1. **Create the Reducer**:

javascript

```javascript
// cartReducer.js
const initialState = {
  items: [],
  total: 0
};

function cartReducer(state = initialState, action) {
  switch (action.type) {
    case 'ADD_ITEM':
      const newItem = action.payload;
      return {
        ...state,
        items: [...state.items, newItem],
        total: state.total + newItem.price
      };
    case 'REMOVE_ITEM':
      const filteredItems = state.items.filter(item => item.id !== action.payload.id);
      const updatedTotal = state.total - action.payload.price;
      return {
        ...state,
```

```
        items: filteredItems,
        total: updatedTotal
      };
    default:
      return state;
  }
}
}


export default cartReducer;
```

2. **Create the Store**:

```
javascript
```

```javascript
// store.js
import { createStore } from 'redux';
import cartReducer from './cartReducer';

const store = createStore(cartReducer);

export default store;
```

Step 2: Create Action Creators

```
javascript
```

```javascript
// cartActions.js
export const addItem = (item) => {
  return {
    type: 'ADD_ITEM',
    payload: item
```

```
  };
};

export const removeItem = (item) => {
  return {
    type: 'REMOVE_ITEM',
    payload: item
  };
};
```

Step 3: Create the React Components

1. **Cart Component**: This component displays the items in the cart and the total price.

javascript

```javascript
// Cart.js
import React from 'react';
import { useSelector } from 'react-redux';

function Cart() {
  const { items, total } = useSelector((state) =>
state);

  return (
    <div>
      <h2>Shopping Cart</h2>
      <ul>
        {items.map((item) => (
```

```
          <li key={item.id}>
            {item.name} - ${item.price}
          </li>
        ))}
      </ul>
      <h3>Total: ${total}</h3>
    </div>
  );
}


export default Cart;
```

2. **Product Component**: This component displays products and allows the user to add them to the cart.

javascript

```
// Product.js
import React from 'react';
import { useDispatch } from 'react-redux';
import { addItem } from './cartActions';

function Product({ product }) {
  const dispatch = useDispatch();

  const handleAddToCart = () => {
    dispatch(addItem(product));
  };

  return (
```

```
    <div>
      <h3>{product.name}</h3>
      <p>${product.price}</p>
      <button  onClick={handleAddToCart}>Add  to
Cart</button>
    </div>
  );
}


export default Product;
```

Step 4: Combine Components in the App

javascript

```javascript
// App.js
import React from 'react';
import { Provider } from 'react-redux';
import store from './store';
import Cart from './Cart';
import Product from './Product';

const products = [
  { id: 1, name: 'Laptop', price: 1000 },
  { id: 2, name: 'Phone', price: 600 },
  { id: 3, name: 'Headphones', price: 150 },
];

function App() {
  return (
    <Provider store={store}>
```

```
<div>
  <h1>Shopping Cart</h1>
  <div>
    {products.map((product) => (
      <Product              key={product.id}
product={product} />
    ))}
  </div>
  <Cart />
</div>
</Provider>
  );
}


export default App;
```

In this example:

- The **Product component** allows users to add items to the cart by dispatching the addItem action.
- The **Cart component** displays the list of items in the cart and the total price. It uses the useSelector hook to access the Redux store.
- The **Redux store** manages the cart state, including the list of items and the total price.

Conclusion

In this chapter, we introduced **Redux** for managing complex state in React applications. We:

- Explained the core concepts of Redux: **actions, reducers**, and the **store**.
- Walked through the process of setting up Redux with React.
- Built a **shopping cart app** where Redux manages the cart state and enables adding/removing items from the cart.

Redux is an essential tool for managing complex state in large applications. It provides a predictable, centralized way to manage data and interact with the state across your app. In the next chapter, we will dive into **asynchronous actions** in Redux, using middleware like **Redux Thunk** to handle API requests and side effects.

CHAPTER 18

ADVANCED REDUX TECHNIQUES

Using Redux Thunk for Handling Asynchronous Actions

One of the common challenges in Redux is dealing with **asynchronous actions**, such as API calls, fetching data from a server, or performing side effects that are not synchronous (e.g., timers, logging, etc.). By default, Redux actions are synchronous, meaning that they are dispatched immediately and return a result. However, in real-world applications, we often need to dispatch actions that don't immediately return a result, such as an API request. This is where **Redux Thunk** comes in.

What is Redux Thunk?

Redux Thunk is a middleware for Redux that allows you to dispatch **functions** instead of plain action objects. These functions can dispatch other actions asynchronously and interact with external APIs or services.

How Redux Thunk Works:

- You dispatch an action creator, but instead of returning an action object, the action creator returns a **function**.
- This function can then perform asynchronous operations (e.g., fetch data from an API), and once the operation is complete, it dispatches actions to update the Redux store.

Installing Redux Thunk

To install **Redux Thunk**, you need to add it as middleware when creating your Redux store:

bash

```
npm install redux-thunk
```

Setting Up Redux Thunk in Your Store:

Here's how to set up Redux Thunk in your Redux store:

1. **Create the Redux Store with Thunk Middleware**:

javascript

```
import { createStore, applyMiddleware } from 'redux';
import thunk from 'redux-thunk';
import rootReducer from './reducers';

const store = createStore(rootReducer, applyMiddleware(thunk));
```

204

```
export default store;
```

- The `applyMiddleware(thunk)` is added to the `createStore` function to enable asynchronous actions.

Optimizing Redux with Reselect and Memoization

As your application grows, the **selectors** that compute derived data from the Redux store can become a bottleneck if they are not optimized. By default, **selectors** in Redux can recompute values on every state change, even if the state values haven't changed. This can lead to unnecessary re-renders and performance issues, especially in large applications.

To solve this, we can use **Reselect**, a selector library for Redux, which provides memoization capabilities to optimize performance by ensuring that derived data is only recomputed when necessary.

What is Reselect?

Reselect is a simple library for **creating selectors** that compute derived data from the Redux store. It automatically memoizes the result of the selector, meaning it only recomputes when the input data changes, reducing unnecessary recalculations.

Installing Reselect:

bash

npm install reselect

Using Reselect for Memoized Selectors:

Here's how to create a memoized selector using Reselect:

1. **Create a Selector**:

javascript

```javascript
import { createSelector } from 'reselect';

// Basic selector to get the cart items
const getCartItems = (state) => state.cart.items;

// Memoized selector to get the total price of
the items in the cart
const getCartTotal = createSelector(
  [getCartItems],  // Inputs
  (items) => items.reduce((total, item) => total
+ item.price, 0) // Output
);
```

- `createSelector` is used to create a selector that computes the total price of the items in the cart.
- The first argument to `createSelector` is an array of input selectors (in this case, `getCartItems`), and the

second argument is a function that computes the derived data (total price).

2. Using the Selector in Components:

To access the memoized selector in your React component, use useSelector from react-redux:

javascript

```
import React from 'react';
import { useSelector } from 'react-redux';
import { getCartTotal } from './selectors';

function CartSummary() {
  const total = useSelector(getCartTotal);

  return <h3>Total: ${total}</h3>;
}

export default CartSummary;
```

With Reselect, the total price will only be recomputed when the items in the cart change. If the cart items are the same, the memoized value is returned, improving performance.

Real-World Example: Enhancing the Shopping Cart with Async Product Fetching

In a real-world shopping cart application, the product data might be fetched from an external API. To implement this, we'll use **Redux Thunk** to handle asynchronous fetching of product data and update the Redux store with the fetched data.

1. Creating Actions for Fetching Products

Here, we'll create async actions that fetch product data and dispatch actions based on the result.

javascript

```javascript
// actions/cartActions.js
import axios from 'axios';

// Action Types
const          FETCH_PRODUCTS_REQUEST          =
'FETCH_PRODUCTS_REQUEST';
const          FETCH_PRODUCTS_SUCCESS          =
'FETCH_PRODUCTS_SUCCESS';
const          FETCH_PRODUCTS_FAILURE          =
'FETCH_PRODUCTS_FAILURE';

// Action Creators
export const fetchProductsRequest = () => ({
  type: FETCH_PRODUCTS_REQUEST
```

```
});


export const fetchProductsSuccess = (products) =>
({
  type: FETCH_PRODUCTS_SUCCESS,
  payload: products
});


export const fetchProductsFailure = (error) => ({
  type: FETCH_PRODUCTS_FAILURE,
  payload: error
});


// Async Action Creator using Redux Thunk
export const fetchProducts = () => {
  return async (dispatch) => {
    dispatch(fetchProductsRequest());
    try {
      const       response       =       await
axios.get('https://api.example.com/products');

dispatch(fetchProductsSuccess(response.data));
    } catch (error) {

dispatch(fetchProductsFailure(error.message));
    }
  };
};
```

- **Actions**:

o   FETCH_PRODUCTS_REQUEST: Dispatched when the product fetching starts.

o   FETCH_PRODUCTS_SUCCESS: Dispatched when the products are successfully fetched.

o   FETCH_PRODUCTS_FAILURE: Dispatched when there's an error fetching the products.

- **Async Action**: The fetchProducts function uses **Redux Thunk** to fetch product data asynchronously and dispatch the appropriate actions.

2. Creating Reducers for Handling Async Data

Now, let's handle the fetched product data in the reducer.

javascript

```javascript
// reducers/cartReducer.js
const initialState = {
  products: [],
  loading: false,
  error: ''
};

function    cartReducer(state    =    initialState,
action) {
  switch (action.type) {
    case 'FETCH_PRODUCTS_REQUEST':
      return { ...state, loading: true };
    case 'FETCH_PRODUCTS_SUCCESS':
```

```
    return  {  ...state,  loading:  false,
products: action.payload };
    case 'FETCH_PRODUCTS_FAILURE':
      return { ...state, loading: false, error:
action.payload };
    default:
      return state;
  }
}


export default cartReducer;
```

- In the reducer, we handle each action (FETCH_PRODUCTS_REQUEST, FETCH_PRODUCTS_SUCCESS, FETCH_PRODUCTS_FAILURE) and update the state accordingly.

3. Connecting Redux to the React Components

Finally, we'll connect the Redux store to our React component and fetch the product data when the component mounts.

```javascript

import React, { useEffect } from 'react';
import { useDispatch, useSelector } from 'react-
redux';
```

211

```jsx
import { fetchProducts } from
'./actions/cartActions';

function ProductList() {
  const dispatch = useDispatch();

  // Accessing state using useSelector
  const { products, loading, error } =
useSelector((state) => state.cart);

  useEffect(() => {
    dispatch(fetchProducts());
  }, [dispatch]);

  if (loading) {
    return <div>Loading products...</div>;
  }

  if (error) {
    return <div>Error: {error}</div>;
  }

  return (
    <div>
      <h2>Product List</h2>
      <ul>
        {products.map((product) => (
          <li key={product.id}>
            {product.name} - ${product.price}
```

```
        </li>
      ))}
    </ul>
  </div>
);
}


export default ProductList;
```

- **useSelector**: We use useSelector to access the products, loading, and error states from Redux.
- **useDispatch**: The useDispatch hook is used to dispatch the fetchProducts action when the component mounts (inside useEffect).
- **Loading and Error States**: We display loading and error messages based on the state.

Conclusion

In this chapter, we explored **advanced Redux techniques** to handle asynchronous actions and optimize performance:

- **Redux Thunk** was introduced as a middleware to handle asynchronous actions, allowing us to fetch data from external APIs and update the Redux store accordingly.
- **Reselect** was used to optimize Redux selectors and improve performance by memoizing computed values.

213

- We built a **shopping cart app** with Redux where products are fetched asynchronously, and the state is managed using Redux.

Redux helps manage complex state in large applications, and with tools like **Redux Thunk** and **Reselect**, you can build highly efficient and scalable apps. In the next chapter, we will explore **React's Context API** and its use for managing global state in React applications.

CHAPTER 19

ERROR BOUNDARIES AND HANDLING ERRORS

Understanding React Error Boundaries for Better Error Handling

In a React application, it's important to ensure that the app remains robust and resilient, even when something goes wrong. Errors can happen at any point during the rendering process, whether from invalid user input, failed API requests, or bugs in the code. React provides a powerful feature called **Error Boundaries** to catch and handle errors gracefully, ensuring that the app does not crash entirely due to unexpected issues.

An **Error Boundary** is a React component that **catches JavaScript errors** anywhere in its child component tree, logs those errors, and displays a fallback UI instead of crashing the whole app. It is used to catch errors during rendering, lifecycle methods, and in the constructors of the whole component tree.

When to Use Error Boundaries:

- To catch errors in **child components** and show a fallback UI instead of letting the entire app crash.

- To catch errors during rendering, in lifecycle methods like `componentDidMount,` and in asynchronous code (like network requests).
- To provide a better **user experience** by displaying a fallback UI (e.g., a loading spinner or error message) instead of a broken page.

Setting Up Error Boundaries in Your App

React provides a special **Error Boundary component** that you can use to wrap parts of your component tree where you want to catch errors. The error boundary component must implement **two lifecycle methods**:

1. **`static getDerivedStateFromError(error)`**: This lifecycle method is invoked when an error is thrown in a child component. It allows you to update the state to trigger a re-render with a fallback UI.

2. **`componentDidCatch(error, info)`**: This method is called after an error is thrown. It's useful for logging the error or sending error details to an error tracking service.

Here's how to create an error boundary component:

1. Create the Error Boundary Component

javascript

```
import React, { Component } from 'react';

class ErrorBoundary extends Component {
  constructor(props) {
    super(props);
    this.state = {
      hasError: false,
      errorInfo: null,
    };
  }

  // This method is invoked when a child
component throws an error
  static getDerivedStateFromError(error) {
    return { hasError: true };
  }

  // This method is called after the error has
been logged
  componentDidCatch(error, info) {
    this.setState({
      errorInfo: info,
    });
    // You can log the error to an external
service
    console.error("Error:", error);
    console.error("Error info:", info);
  }
```

```
render() {
  if (this.state.hasError) {
    // Fallback UI
    return (
      <div>
        <h1>Something went wrong.</h1>
        <p>We are working on fixing it!</p>
      </div>
    );
  }

  // Render children if no error
  return this.props.children;
  }
}

export default ErrorBoundary;
```

Explanation:

- **getDerivedStateFromError**: This lifecycle method sets the state hasError to true when an error is thrown, indicating that the error boundary should display the fallback UI.
- **componentDidCatch**: This method is useful for logging the error to an external service or console. It also allows us to capture detailed error information.

218

2. Using Error Boundaries in Your App

Now that we have the `ErrorBoundary` component, you can wrap your child components to catch errors in those components.

javascript

```javascript
import React, { Component } from 'react';
import ErrorBoundary from './ErrorBoundary';

class Product extends Component {
  render() {
    if (this.props.product === null) {
      throw new Error("Product not found!"); // Simulate an error
    }

    return <div>{this.props.product.name}</div>;
  }
}

class App extends Component {
  render() {
    return (
      <div>
        <h1>Product List</h1>
        <ErrorBoundary>
          <Product product={{ name: 'Product A' }} />
```

```
        <Product  product={null}  />  {/*  This
will trigger an error */}
      </ErrorBoundary>
    </div>
  );
 }
}


export default App;
```

Explanation:

- In the `App` component, we use the `ErrorBoundary` component to wrap the `Product` components.
- One of the `Product` components intentionally throws an error by passing `null` as the product (to simulate a missing product).
- The error boundary catches the error and renders the fallback UI (`Something went wrong.`) instead of crashing the entire app.

Example: Handling UI Errors Gracefully with Error Boundaries

Let's walk through a more practical example where we fetch data asynchronously and display a list of items. If there is an error fetching the data, we will handle it gracefully using an error boundary.

Step 1: Create the Data Fetching Component

javascript

```javascript
import React, { useState, useEffect } from 'react';

function ProductList() {
  const [products, setProducts] = useState([]);
  const [loading, setLoading] = useState(true);
  const [error, setError] = useState(null);

  useEffect(() => {
    fetch('https://api.example.com/products')
      .then((response) => response.json())
      .then((data) => {
        setProducts(data);
        setLoading(false);
      })
      .catch((error) => {
        setError('Failed to load products');
        setLoading(false);
      });
  }, []);

  if (loading) {
    return <div>Loading...</div>;
  }

  if (error) {
```

```
    throw new Error(error); // Simulating an
error if fetching fails
  }

  return (
    <ul>
      {products.map((product) => (
        <li key={product.id}>{product.name}</li>
      ))}
    </ul>
  );
}

export default ProductList;
```

Step 2: Wrap with Error Boundary in App

Now, let's wrap the `ProductList` component with an `ErrorBoundary` in the `App` component.

javascript

```
import React from 'react';
import ErrorBoundary from './ErrorBoundary';
import ProductList from './ProductList';

function App() {
  return (
    <div>
      <h1>Product List</h1>
```

```
    <ErrorBoundary>
      <ProductList />
    </ErrorBoundary>
  </div>
  );
}
```

```
export default App;
```

Explanation:

- **ProductList Component**: Fetches product data from an API and displays it in a list. If there's an error (e.g., network failure), an error is thrown.
- **ErrorBoundary Component**: Catches the error and displays a user-friendly message (Something went wrong.) without crashing the whole app.

Best Practices for Error Boundaries

- **Use Error Boundaries for Large Components**: Wrap large parts of your application (e.g., complex UI components, feature-specific components) in error boundaries to isolate errors and prevent them from affecting the entire app.
- **Use Fallback UI**: When rendering the fallback UI in an error boundary, make sure it's clear to the user that

something went wrong and provide a way to recover, such as a retry button.

- **Global Error Boundaries**: You can place a global error boundary around your entire app, but it's generally better to wrap smaller parts of the app to handle errors more granularly.

Conclusion

In this chapter, we learned about **React Error Boundaries** and how to use them for **graceful error handling**. Key concepts included:

- **Error Boundaries** catch errors in the component tree, display fallback UI, and prevent the app from crashing.
- We saw how to set up an error boundary by using the `getDerivedStateFromError` and `componentDidCatch` methods.
- We implemented a **real-world example** of handling errors during data fetching and displaying a fallback UI when errors occur.

Error boundaries are an essential tool for building robust, user-friendly applications in React. They help ensure that errors in one part of the app do not bring down the entire application. In the next chapter, we will explore **testing** React components, including best practices for unit tests and integration tests.

CHAPTER 20

TESTING REACT COMPONENTS

Introduction to Testing with Jest and React Testing Library

Testing is a crucial aspect of the software development process. It helps ensure that the application behaves as expected, that bugs are caught early, and that future changes don't inadvertently break existing functionality. In React, testing can be done at different levels: unit testing, integration testing, and end-to-end testing.

In this chapter, we will focus on **unit testing** React components using **Jest** and **React Testing Library**. These tools are commonly used for testing React applications because they provide a simple and powerful way to write tests for individual components and hooks.

What is Jest?

- **Jest** is a popular testing framework that comes with a lot of built-in functionality, including running tests, mocking modules, and assertion utilities. Jest is often used with React applications because it integrates well with React Testing Library.

What is React Testing Library?

- **React Testing Library** is a library that makes it easier to test React components by encouraging good testing practices. It focuses on testing components the way users interact with them, rather than testing implementation details.

Together, Jest and React Testing Library provide a robust solution for testing React components.

Writing Unit Tests for Components and Hooks

Unit tests focus on testing the smallest pieces of your application in isolation. In React, this usually means testing components or hooks independently from the rest of the app. The goal of unit testing is to ensure that each part of the app works as expected.

1. Testing React Components

A **React component** is typically tested by rendering it in a test environment, simulating user interactions, and asserting that the component's behavior is correct.

Steps for Testing React Components:

1. **Render the component**: Use the `render()` function from React Testing Library to render the component into a test container.

2. **Simulate user interactions**: Use the `fireEvent` utility to simulate user events (clicks, typing, etc.).

3. **Assert the behavior**: Use assertions (like `expect`) to check that the component behaves as expected.

2. Testing React Hooks

Testing **custom hooks** requires a slightly different approach since hooks don't have a UI to interact with. React Testing Library provides a utility called `renderHook` to render and test hooks directly.

Real-World Example: Writing Tests for a Form Component

Let's build a **form component** with validation and write tests for it. The form will have two fields: email and password. We will validate the fields on submit and show error messages if the fields are empty or the email is not in the correct format.

Step 1: Create the Form Component
javascript

```javascript
import React, { useState } from 'react';
```

```
function SignUpForm() {
  const [email, setEmail] = useState('');
  const [password, setPassword] = useState('');
  const [error, setError] = useState('');

  const validateEmail = (email) => {
    const re = /^[a-zA-Z0-9._-]+@[a-zA-Z0-9.-
]+\.[a-zA-Z]{2,6}$/;
    return re.test(email);
  };

  const handleSubmit = (event) => {
    event.preventDefault();

    if (!email || !password) {
      setError('All fields are required');
    } else if (!validateEmail(email)) {
      setError('Invalid email format');
    } else {
      setError('');
      // Simulate successful form submission
      alert('Form submitted!');
    }
  };

  return (
    <form onSubmit={handleSubmit}>
      <div>
        <label>Email:</label>
```

```
        <input
          type="email"
          value={email}
          onChange={(e)                          =>
setEmail(e.target.value)}
          data-testid="email-input"
        />
      </div>
      <div>
        <label>Password:</label>
        <input
          type="password"
          value={password}
          onChange={(e)                          =>
setPassword(e.target.value)}
          data-testid="password-input"
        />
      </div>
      {error && <div data-testid="error-message"
style={{ color: 'red' }}>{error}</div>}
      <button type="submit">Submit</button>
    </form>
  );
}


export default SignUpForm;
```

In this component:

- We use `useState` to manage the `email`, `password`, and `error` states.

- The `handleSubmit` function validates the form and displays an error message if the fields are invalid.

- The form will submit successfully if both the email and password are provided and the email is in a valid format.

Step 2: Write Unit Tests for the Form Component

Now, let's write tests for the `SignUpForm` component.

1. **Install Dependencies**:

   If you haven't already installed **Jest** and **React Testing Library**, install them using the following command:

   ```bash
   npm install --save-dev @testing-library/react @testing-library/jest-dom jest
   ```

2. **Create the Test File**:

```javascript
import { render, screen, fireEvent } from '@testing-library/react';
import SignUpForm from './SignUpForm';
```

231

```
describe('SignUpForm', () => {
  test('renders the form fields', () => {
    render(<SignUpForm />);

    // Check if the form fields are rendered

expect(screen.getByLabelText(/email/i)).toBeInT
heDocument();

expect(screen.getByLabelText(/password/i)).toBe
InTheDocument();
    expect(screen.getByRole('button',  {   name:
/submit/i })).toBeInTheDocument();
  });

  test('shows error when email is empty', () =>
{
    render(<SignUpForm />);

    // Simulate form submission with empty fields
    fireEvent.click(screen.getByRole('button', {
name: /submit/i }));

    // Check for error message
    expect(screen.getByTestId('error-
message')).toHaveTextContent('All  fields  are
required');
  });
```

```
test('shows    error    when    email    format    is
invalid', () => {
    render(<SignUpForm />);

    // Fill in the form with an invalid email
    fireEvent.change(screen.getByTestId('email-
input'), { target: { value: 'invalidemail' } });

fireEvent.change(screen.getByTestId('password-
input'), { target: { value: 'password123' } });
    fireEvent.click(screen.getByRole('button', {
name: /submit/i }));

    // Check for error message
    expect(screen.getByTestId('error-
message')).toHaveTextContent('Invalid       email
format');
  });

  test('submits the form successfully when fields
are valid', () => {
    render(<SignUpForm />);

    // Fill in the form with valid data
    fireEvent.change(screen.getByTestId('email-
input'), { target: { value: 'test@example.com' }
});
```

```
fireEvent.change(screen.getByTestId('password-
input'), { target: { value: 'password123' } });

    // Mock alert to test successful submission
    window.alert = jest.fn();

    // Simulate form submission
    fireEvent.click(screen.getByRole('button', {
name: /submit/i }));

    // Check if the alert was called

expect(window.alert).toHaveBeenCalledWith('Form
submitted!');
  });
});
```

Explanation of the Tests:

1. **Render Test**: The first test ensures that the form fields (email, password, and submit button) are rendered correctly.

2. **Error Handling Test (Empty Fields)**: This test simulates submitting the form with empty fields and ensures that the appropriate error message is displayed.

3. **Error Handling Test (Invalid Email Format)**: This test simulates submitting the form with an invalid email

format and ensures that the appropriate error message is displayed.

4. **Successful Submission Test**: This test simulates submitting the form with valid data and checks that the form is submitted successfully (by checking that the `alert` function is called).

Conclusion

In this chapter, we learned how to **test React components** using **Jest** and **React Testing Library**. Key takeaways include:

- **Unit testing** components and ensuring that their behavior is correct.

- Using **Jest** to mock functions like `alert` and check if they are called during form submission.

- Testing various edge cases, such as invalid input and empty form fields, to ensure that errors are handled gracefully.

- Leveraging **React Testing Library** to query DOM elements in a way that simulates how users interact with the application.

Testing is a critical part of React development that helps ensure that components work as expected and reduces the likelihood of bugs. In the next chapter, we will explore **end-to-end testing** with

Cypress, which allows you to test your entire application, including the front-end and back-end, in a real browser environment.

CHAPTER 21

WORKING WITH WEBPACK AND BABEL

Understanding the Role of Webpack and Babel in React Projects

In modern web development, tools like **Webpack** and **Babel** play crucial roles in building and optimizing JavaScript applications. For React projects, these tools are used to bundle and transpile the code, enabling you to work with the latest JavaScript features, such as **ES6 modules**, **JSX syntax**, and **React-specific features**. Let's explore each tool's role in React projects.

1. What is Webpack?

Webpack is a **module bundler**. It takes modules (JavaScript files, CSS files, images, etc.) and bundles them into one or more **bundles** that can be loaded by the browser. Webpack allows you to efficiently manage assets, optimize performance, and load dependencies in a structured manner.

Key Features of Webpack:

- **Module Bundling**: Combines multiple files (JavaScript, CSS, images) into one or more optimized bundles.

- **Code Splitting**: Allows splitting the code into smaller chunks that are loaded on demand, improving load time.
- **Loaders and Plugins**: Webpack uses **loaders** to transform files before bundling (e.g., transpiling JavaScript or processing styles) and **plugins** to perform tasks like minification and optimizing the output.

2. What is Babel?

Babel is a **JavaScript compiler** that allows you to use modern JavaScript features (like ES6, ES7, JSX) while ensuring compatibility with older browsers. Babel transpiles newer JavaScript code into a version of JavaScript that can run in older browsers.

For React, Babel also handles **JSX syntax** and converts it into standard JavaScript that the browser can understand.

Key Features of Babel:

- **Transpiling**: Converts modern JavaScript (ES6+) into backwards-compatible JavaScript (ES5).
- **JSX Support**: Converts JSX code into React.createElement calls, allowing you to write JSX syntax in React.
- **Plugins and Presets**: Babel uses plugins and presets to transform specific features like async/await or arrow functions.

Setting Up a React Project with Webpack and Babel

To set up a React project with Webpack and Babel, we need to install and configure both tools. This involves several steps, including installing dependencies, configuring Webpack to handle React code, and setting up Babel to transpile JSX and modern JavaScript.

Step 1: Create the Project Folder

Create a new folder for your project and navigate into it.

bash

```
mkdir react-webpack-babel
cd react-webpack-babel
```

Step 2: Initialize the Project

Initialize the project with `npm init` to create a `package.json` file.

bash

```
npm init -y
```

Step 3: Install Dependencies

Next, install the necessary dependencies for React, Webpack, and Babel.

1. **React and ReactDOM** (for building the app):

bash

```
npm install react react-dom
```

2. **Webpack and related packages** (for bundling the app):

bash

```
npm install --save-dev webpack webpack-cli
webpack-dev-server html-webpack-plugin
```

3. **Babel and related packages** (for transpiling JSX and modern JavaScript):

bash

```
npm install --save-dev babel-loader @babel/core
@babel/preset-env @babel/preset-react
```

4. **CSS and file loaders** (for handling styles and assets):

bash

```
npm install --save-dev style-loader css-loader
```

Step 4: Set Up Webpack Configuration

Create a file called `webpack.config.js` in the root of your project. This file will configure Webpack for your React app.

```javascript
const path = require('path');
const HtmlWebpackPlugin = require('html-webpack-plugin');

module.exports = {
  entry: './src/index.js', // Entry point of the app
  output: {
    path: path.resolve(__dirname, 'dist'),
    filename: 'bundle.js', // Output bundle file
  },
  module: {
    rules: [
      {
        test: /\.js$/, // All .js files
        exclude: /node_modules/,
        use: {
          loader: 'babel-loader', // Use Babel to transpile JavaScript
        },
      },
```

241

```
      {
        test: /\.css$/, // All .css files
        use: ['style-loader', 'css-loader'], //
Load styles
      },
    ],
  },
  plugins: [
    new HtmlWebpackPlugin({
      template: './public/index.html', // HTML
template to inject the bundle
    }),
  ],
  devServer: {
    contentBase: path.join(__dirname, 'dist'),
    port: 3000, // Local dev server on port 3000
    hot: true,
  },
};
```

Explanation:

- **Entry**: The `entry` point specifies where Webpack starts bundling your app (in this case, `./src/index.js`).
- **Output**: The `output` section defines where the bundled file (`bundle.js`) will be stored.
- **Loaders**: We use `babel-loader` to transpile `.js` files and handle JSX syntax, and `style-loader` and `css-loader` to handle CSS files.

242

- **Plugins**: `HtmlWebpackPlugin` is used to inject the bundled JavaScript file into an HTML template.
- **DevServer**: This configures Webpack's development server, enabling hot reloading and serving the app locally.

Step 5: Set Up Babel Configuration

Create a `.babelrc` file in the root of your project to specify Babel presets.

json

```json
{
  "presets":                    ["@babel/preset-env",
"@babel/preset-react"]
}
```

- **@babel/preset-env**: Transpiles modern JavaScript features to compatible JavaScript for older browsers.
- **@babel/preset-react**: Transpiles JSX into `React.createElement` calls.

Step 6: Set Up the React App

Create the `src` folder and an `index.js` file inside it to write your React code.

1. **Create src/index.js**:

javascript

```javascript
import React from 'react';
import ReactDOM from 'react-dom';
import './index.css';

function App() {
  return <h1>Hello, Webpack and Babel!</h1>;
}

ReactDOM.render(<App />,
document.getElementById('root'));
```

2. **Create public/index.html:**

html

```html
<!DOCTYPE html>
<html lang="en">
  <head>
    <meta charset="UTF-8" />
    <title>React Webpack Babel</title>
  </head>
  <body>
    <div id="root"></div>
  </body>
</html>
```

This is the HTML template where the React app will be injected by Webpack.

244

Step 7: Update `package.json` for Scripts

In `package.json`, add the following scripts to start the development server and build the app:

json

```
{
  "scripts": {
    "start": "webpack serve --mode development -
-open", // Start the development server
    "build": "webpack --mode production" // Build
the app for production
  }
}
```

Example: Customizing Webpack for React Apps

Once you have set up Webpack, you can further customize your configuration for more advanced features. Here are some common customizations you might need:

1. Adding CSS and Image Support

To support images, fonts, and other static assets, add a loader to handle file imports.

1. **Install File Loader**:

```bash
bash

npm install --save-dev file-loader
```

2. **Update Webpack Configuration**:

```javascript
javascript

module: {
  rules: [
    {
      test: /\.js$/,
      exclude: /node_modules/,
      use: {
        loader: 'babel-loader',
      },
    },
    {
      test: /\.css$/,
      use: ['style-loader', 'css-loader'],
    },
    {
      test: /\.(png|svg|jpg|jpeg|gif)$/i,
      use: ['file-loader'], // Handle image files
    },
  ],
},
```

2. Adding Source Maps for Debugging

Source maps help you debug your React app by mapping the minified code back to the original source code. To enable source maps in development:

javascript

```
module.exports = {
  // other configurations...
  devtool: 'source-map',
};
```

Conclusion

In this chapter, we:

- **Explored the roles of Webpack and Babel** in React projects, understanding how they bundle and transpile code.
- **Set up a React project** with Webpack and Babel to handle JavaScript, JSX, and CSS.
- **Customized Webpack** to add features like handling images, source maps, and production builds.

Webpack and Babel are crucial tools for modern web development, and understanding how to configure and customize them will allow you to build efficient and optimized React applications.

In the next chapter, we will explore **React performance optimization techniques**, including lazy loading, code splitting, and memoization to improve the performance of large-scale React apps.

CHAPTER 22

SERVER-SIDE RENDERING (SSR) WITH REACT

Introduction to Server-Side Rendering and Its Benefits for SEO

Server-Side Rendering (SSR) refers to the process where HTML pages are generated on the server and sent to the client. This is in contrast to **Client-Side Rendering (CSR)**, where JavaScript runs in the browser to render the content. SSR is often used to improve the **initial load time** and **SEO performance** of a web application, especially for **React** apps, which are typically rendered on the client-side by default.

Benefits of SSR:

1. **Improved SEO**:
   o Search engine crawlers have difficulty reading JavaScript-heavy websites. SSR helps by serving fully rendered HTML, which is easier for search engines to index, thus improving search rankings.
   o Pages are pre-rendered on the server with their content, making it more accessible to search engine bots.

2. **Faster Initial Load**:

   o Since the HTML is pre-rendered on the server and delivered to the client, the browser can display the content immediately without waiting for JavaScript to load and render the page.

3. **Better User Experience**:

   o With faster initial rendering, the user can see content more quickly, leading to a smoother experience.

   o Especially beneficial for mobile users with slower internet connections.

4. **Sharing and Social Media Integration**:

   o When sharing links on social media, SSR ensures that the full page content (including metadata like titles and descriptions) is available for preview, improving social sharing capabilities.

Setting Up React for Server-Side Rendering with Express

Setting up **SSR** with **React** and **Express** involves a few steps. The basic flow is:

1. **React** components are rendered on the server using Node.js.

2. The HTML content generated on the server is sent to the client.

3. React then takes over on the client-side (known as **hydration**) to make the page interactive.

Step 1: Install Required Dependencies

First, let's set up a project by installing the necessary dependencies.

1. Create a new folder for your project and navigate into it.

   bash

   ```bash
   mkdir react-ssr
   cd react-ssr
   ```

2. Initialize a new Node.js project.

   bash

   ```bash
   npm init -y
   ```

3. Install **React**, **ReactDOM**, **Express**, and **ReactDOMServer**.

   bash

   ```bash
   npm install react react-dom express react-dom/server
   ```

251

- o react-dom/server: This package allows you to render React components on the server.
- o express: A lightweight web server to serve our React app on the server.

Step 2: Set Up Express for SSR

Now let's create the server using Express that will handle SSR. Create a file called server.js in the root of your project.

1. **Create server.js:**

javascript

```javascript
import express from 'express';
import React from 'react';
import ReactDOMServer from 'react-dom/server';
import App from './src/App';

const app = express();

// Serve static files from the "public" directory
app.use(express.static('public'));

// Handle requests to the root route by rendering
the React app server-side
app.get('/', (req, res) => {
  // Render the React app to a string
```

```
const                    content                    =
ReactDOMServer.renderToString(<App />);

  // Send the full HTML to the client
  res.send(`
    <!DOCTYPE html>
    <html lang="en">
      <head>
        <meta charset="UTF-8">
        <meta                    name="viewport"
content="width=device-width, initial-scale=1.0">
        <title>React SSR</title>
      </head>
      <body>
        <div id="root">${content}</div>
        <script src="/bundle.js"></script>
      </body>
    </html>
  `);
});

// Start the server on port 3000
app.listen(3000, () => {
  console.log('Server      is      running      on
http://localhost:3000');
});
```

- **express.static** serves static files like JavaScript and CSS, which we will build later.

253

- **ReactDOMServer.renderToString()** renders the React component into a string of HTML that can be inserted into the response.
- The server sends an HTML response with the fully rendered content.

Step 3: Set Up React Components

Now, let's create a simple React component that we will render on the server.

1. **Create src/App.js:**

javascript

```javascript
import React from 'react';

function App() {
  return (
    <div>
      <h1>Hello, SSR with React and Express!</h1>
      <p>This page is server-rendered.</p>
    </div>
  );
}

export default App;
```

- This simple component will display a header and some text. It will be rendered on the server and sent as part of the initial HTML.

Step 4: Bundle the Client-Side Code

In order to make the page interactive once it's loaded on the client, we need to "hydrate" the app using React on the client-side. To do this, we need to bundle the client-side code using **Webpack**.

1. **Install Webpack and Babel**:

bash

```
npm install --save-dev webpack webpack-cli
webpack-node-externals babel-loader @babel/core
@babel/preset-env @babel/preset-react
```

- **webpack**: Bundles your JavaScript files for the browser.
- **babel-loader**: Allows Babel to transpile JavaScript and JSX.
- **@babel/preset-env** and **@babel/preset-react**: Presets for transpiling modern JavaScript and JSX.

2. **Create the Webpack Configuration File**:

Create a file named webpack.config.js for bundling the client-side code.

```javascript
const path = require('path');

module.exports = {
  entry: './src/index.js', // Entry point for client-side code
  output: {
    filename: 'bundle.js',
    path: path.resolve(__dirname, 'public'),
  },
  module: {
    rules: [
      {
        test: /\.js$/,
        exclude: /node_modules/,
        use: 'babel-loader', // Transpile JavaScript and JSX
      },
    ],
  },
  resolve: {
    extensions: ['.js', '.jsx'],
  },
};
```

- This configuration tells Webpack to bundle the code starting from src/index.js and output it as bundle.js in the public folder.

256

3. Create `src/index.js` for Client-Side Hydration:

javascript

```javascript
import React from 'react';
import ReactDOM from 'react-dom';
import App from './App';

// Hydrate the app on the client-side
ReactDOM.hydrate(<App                    />,
document.getElementById('root'));
```

- `ReactDOM.hydrate` is used to attach event listeners and other client-side behavior to the HTML that was pre-rendered by the server.

4. Add Babel Configuration:

Create a `.babelrc` file to specify Babel presets:

json

```json
{
  "presets":                ["@babel/preset-env",
"@babel/preset-react"]
}
```

5. Update `package.json` Scripts:

257

In `package.json`, add the following scripts to build and start the server:

json

```json
{
  "scripts": {
    "start": "node server.js",    // Start the
Express server
    "build": "webpack --mode production",    //
Build client-side bundle
    "dev": "webpack --mode development --watch"
// Watch for changes in development
  }
}
```

Real-World Example: Creating a Basic SSR App with React and Express

Now, let's run the full stack:

1. **Run the server**:

Start the server using the following command:

bash

```bash
npm start
```

2. **Build the client-side code**:

In another terminal window, build the client-side code using Webpack:

```bash
```

```
npm run build
```

3. **Access the App**:

Open your browser and visit `http://localhost:3000`. You should see the pre-rendered content (`Hello, SSR with React and Express!`) that was generated by the server. Once the JavaScript is loaded, React will "hydrate" the app, making it interactive.

Conclusion

In this chapter, we explored **Server-Side Rendering (SSR)** with React and Express. We:

- Discussed the **benefits of SSR**, such as improved SEO and faster initial load times.
- Set up a **React app for SSR** with Express by rendering components on the server and sending them as HTML.

- Learned how to **hydrate the app on the client** to make it interactive using React.

SSR is a great approach for improving the performance and SEO of React applications, especially for content-heavy websites. In the next chapter, we will dive into **static site generation (SSG)** and how it compares to SSR for certain types of web apps.

CHAPTER 23

REACT AND MOBILE DEVELOPMENT WITH REACT NATIVE

Introduction to React Native for Building Mobile Apps

React Native is a powerful framework developed by Facebook that allows developers to build **mobile applications** using **JavaScript** and **React**. With React Native, you can write mobile apps for both **iOS** and **Android** using the same codebase, making it an excellent choice for building cross-platform applications.

React Native allows you to write components using familiar React syntax but renders them using native mobile components rather than web components. This means that you can leverage the power of **React's declarative UI components** and **JavaScript's flexibility** to create mobile apps that are nearly indistinguishable from apps built using native technologies like Swift for iOS or Java for Android.

261

Why Choose React Native?

- **Cross-Platform Development**: React Native enables you to write apps for both iOS and Android using a single codebase, saving time and effort.
- **Hot Reloading**: You can immediately see changes you make to your code, speeding up the development process.
- **Native Performance**: React Native allows you to write components that are rendered using native mobile views, providing performance close to that of native apps.
- **Wide Community Support**: React Native has a large, active community, providing ample resources, libraries, and plugins to help you during development.

Key Differences Between React for the Web and React Native

While **React** for the web and **React Native** share many similarities (both use React's declarative syntax, component-based architecture, and state management), there are key differences due to the distinct nature of mobile development. Let's explore the main differences:

1. Components:

- **React (Web)**: Uses HTML elements like `<div>`, `<span>`, `<button>`, etc.

262

- **React Native**: Uses mobile-specific components, such as `<View>`, `<Text>`, `<Button>`, and `<Image>`. These components are similar to HTML elements but are designed for mobile interfaces.

2. Styling:

- **React (Web)**: Styles are applied using **CSS** or **CSS-in-JS** libraries like styled-components.
- **React Native**: Styling is done using a **JavaScript object** that mimics CSS properties, but it uses a mobile-optimized layout system based on **Flexbox**. There are no external CSS files in React Native, and styles are applied directly within the component files.

```javascript
// Example of React Native styling
const styles = {
  container: {
    flex: 1,
    justifyContent: 'center',
    alignItems: 'center',
    backgroundColor: 'lightblue',
  },
};
```

3. Navigation:

- **React (Web)**: Uses browser-based routing (e.g., `React Router`) for navigation.
- **React Native**: Uses libraries like `React Navigation` or `React Native Navigation` to handle navigation between screens.

4. Native Modules:

- **React (Web)**: Accesses browser APIs for tasks like geolocation, local storage, etc.
- **React Native**: Has access to mobile device features such as the camera, GPS, contacts, and other native APIs via **native modules**.

5. Performance:

- **React (Web)**: Renders content in the browser, which is a little slower compared to native rendering.
- **React Native**: Renders using native components, providing a performance closer to that of native apps.

Example: Building a Simple To-Do App for Mobile with React Native

Let's build a basic **To-Do App** using **React Native**. This app will allow users to add and remove tasks. The app will include basic functionality such as adding tasks, marking them as complete, and deleting tasks.

Step 1: Setting Up the Environment

Before we start, ensure you have the necessary tools to build React Native apps:

1. Install **Node.js** from nodejs.org.
2. Install **Expo CLI** globally (for easier setup and running of React Native apps):

bash

```
npm install -g expo-cli
```

3. Create a new React Native project using Expo:

bash

```
expo init TodoApp
```

4. Choose a template (e.g., **blank**), and navigate into the project directory:

```bash
```

```
cd TodoApp
```

5. Start the development server:

```bash
```

```
expo start
```

This will open the Expo developer tools in your browser. You can use an **Android Emulator**, **iOS Simulator**, or the **Expo Go app** on your mobile device to view the app.

Step 2: Building the To-Do App

Now, let's implement the To-Do app with simple functionality.

1. **Create App.js** and add the following code:

```javascript
```

```javascript
import React, { useState } from 'react';
import { View, Text, TextInput, Button, FlatList,
StyleSheet } from 'react-native';

export default function App() {
  const [task, setTask] = useState('');
  const [tasks, setTasks] = useState([]);
```

```
// Add a new task
const addTask = () => {
  if (task) {
    setTasks([...tasks,          {          id:
Math.random().toString(), text: task }]);
    setTask(''); // Clear input field after
adding
  }
};

// Remove a task
const removeTask = (id) => {
  setTasks(tasks.filter((task) => task.id !==
id));
  };

return (
  <View style={styles.container}>
    <Text          style={styles.header}>To-Do
App</Text>
    <TextInput
      style={styles.input}
      placeholder="Add a new task"
      value={task}
      onChangeText={setTask}
    />
    <Button title="Add Task" onPress={addTask}
/>
    <FlatList
```

267

```
      data={tasks}
      renderItem={({ item }) => (
        <View style={styles.taskItem}>
          <Text>{item.text}</Text>
          <Button title="Delete" onPress={()
=> removeTask(item.id)} />
        </View>
      )}
      keyExtractor={(item) => item.id}
    />
  </View>
  );
}


const styles = StyleSheet.create({
  container: {
    flex: 1,
    paddingTop: 50,
    paddingHorizontal: 20,
    backgroundColor: '#f0f0f0',
  },
  header: {
    fontSize: 24,
    fontWeight: 'bold',
    textAlign: 'center',
    marginBottom: 20,
  },
  input: {
    height: 40,
```

```
    borderColor: 'gray',
    borderWidth: 1,
    marginBottom: 20,
    paddingLeft: 10,
  },
  taskItem: {
    flexDirection: 'row',
    justifyContent: 'space-between',
    padding: 10,
    borderBottomWidth: 1,
    borderColor: '#ccc',
  },
});
```

Explanation:

- **State Management**: We use the `useState` hook to manage two pieces of state:
  o `task`: The value of the input field.
  o `tasks`: An array to store the list of tasks.
- **Adding Tasks**: The `addTask` function adds a new task to the `tasks` array and clears the input field.
- **Removing Tasks**: The `removeTask` function removes a task from the list by filtering out the task with the specified ID.
- **Rendering Tasks**: We use **FlatList** to render the tasks. This is an optimized way to display lists in React Native.
- **Styling**: React Native uses **StyleSheet** to define styles, similar to CSS but using JavaScript objects.

269

Step 3: Running the App

Once you've added the code, you can run the app on your emulator or device:

1. Launch the app using Expo by running `expo start` in the terminal.
2. Scan the QR code with the **Expo Go app** on your mobile device or run the app on an emulator.

You should see the basic To-Do app with functionality to add and remove tasks. The UI is rendered using native components such as `View`, `Text`, `TextInput`, and `Button`.

Conclusion

In this chapter, we explored how to use **React Native** to build mobile applications. Key takeaways include:

- **React Native** allows you to use React to build cross-platform mobile apps for both iOS and Android.
- The key differences between **React for the web** and **React Native**, including components, styling, and navigation.
- A hands-on example of building a **simple To-Do app** for mobile using React Native, showcasing the core features

such as state management, rendering lists, and handling user input.

React Native is an excellent choice for building high-quality mobile apps using the same concepts and libraries as React. In the next chapter, we will dive deeper into **navigation in React Native** and explore how to manage app navigation with libraries like **React Navigation**.

CHAPTER 24

MANAGING MOBILE STATE IN REACT NATIVE

Using State Management Techniques in React Native Apps

State management in **React Native** is similar to **React** for the web, but there are additional challenges to consider due to the mobile platform. Managing the state effectively in React Native apps is crucial for providing a smooth user experience, especially when the app becomes more complex.

React Native apps rely on the same fundamental state management techniques as React, such as **local component state**, **Context API**, and **Redux**, but they may also include mobile-specific concerns like network requests, device-specific data, and managing multiple screens.

State Management Techniques in React Native:

1. **Local Component State**: For small apps or components, you can manage state using React's built-in `useState` hook or the older `this.setState` in class components.

2. **Context API**: The **Context API** is ideal for managing global state in smaller apps or when you need to pass data deeply through the component tree without prop drilling.

3. **Redux**: **Redux** is a more powerful solution for managing complex state in larger apps. It centralizes the state and makes it easier to manage global state and handle side effects.

In this chapter, we will focus on using **Redux** in React Native to manage the state in a larger application, as it is especially useful for **large-scale apps** where state needs to be shared across multiple screens and components.

Leveraging Redux in React Native

Redux is a popular state management library for JavaScript applications, including React and React Native apps. It helps manage the app's state in a predictable way, making it easier to track and debug state changes.

Key Concepts of Redux:

- **Store**: A centralized place where the entire app's state is stored.
- **Actions**: Plain JavaScript objects that describe an event or action that occurred (e.g., adding a to-do item).

- **Reducers**: Functions that determine how the app's state changes based on actions.
- **Dispatch**: A method used to send actions to the Redux store to update the state.

Setting Up Redux in React Native:

1. **Install Redux and React-Redux**:

bash

```
npm install redux react-redux
```

2. **Create Actions**: Define actions that describe state changes.

javascript

```
// actions/todoActions.js
export const addTodo = (todo) => {
  return {
    type: 'ADD_TODO',
    payload: todo,
  };
};

export const removeTodo = (id) => {
  return {
    type: 'REMOVE_TODO',
```

```javascript
    payload: id,
  };
};
```

3. **Create Reducers**: Define how the state will change in response to actions.

javascript

```javascript
// reducers/todoReducer.js
const initialState = {
  todos: [],
};

function todoReducer(state = initialState,
action) {
  switch (action.type) {
    case 'ADD_TODO':
      return {
        ...state,
        todos: [...state.todos, action.payload],
      };
    case 'REMOVE_TODO':
      return {
        ...state,
        todos:   state.todos.filter((todo)   =>
todo.id !== action.payload),
      };
    default:
      return state;
```

```
    }
}
```

```
export default todoReducer;
```

4. **Create the Redux Store**: Set up the Redux store to manage the app's state.

javascript

```
// store.js
import { createStore } from 'redux';
import            todoReducer            from
'./reducers/todoReducer';

const store = createStore(todoReducer);

export default store;
```

5. **Connect Redux to React Native**: Use the `Provider` component from `react-redux` to connect the store to the app.

javascript

```
// index.js
import React from 'react';
import { AppRegistry } from 'react-native';
import { Provider } from 'react-redux';
import App from './App';
```

```javascript
import store from './store';
import { name as appName } from './app.json';

AppRegistry.registerComponent(appName, () => (
  <Provider store={store}>
    <App />
  </Provider>
));
```

6. **Accessing Redux State in Components**: Use `useSelector` to read state and `useDispatch` to dispatch actions in your components.

javascript

```javascript
// TodoList.js
import React from 'react';
import { View, Text, Button, FlatList } from 'react-native';
import { useSelector, useDispatch } from 'react-redux';
import { addTodo, removeTodo } from './actions/todoActions';

function TodoList() {
  const dispatch = useDispatch();
  const todos = useSelector((state) => state.todos);
```

```
const handleAddTodo = () => {
  const      newTodo      =      {      id:
Math.random().toString(), text: 'New To-Do' };
    dispatch(addTodo(newTodo));
  };

  const handleRemoveTodo = (id) => {
    dispatch(removeTodo(id));
  };

  return (
    <View>
      <Button          title="Add          Todo"
onPress={handleAddTodo} />
      <FlatList
        data={todos}
        keyExtractor={(item) => item.id}
        renderItem={({ item }) => (
          <View>
            <Text>{item.text}</Text>
            <Button   title="Remove"   onPress={()
=> handleRemoveTodo(item.id)} />
          </View>
        )}
      />
    </View>
  );
}
```

```
export default TodoList;
```

Explanation of the Code:

- **useSelector**: This hook allows us to access the Redux store's state (in this case, the `todos` array).
- **useDispatch**: This hook allows us to dispatch actions (e.g., `addTodo` and `removeTodo`) to update the Redux store.
- **Rendering the To-Do List**: The `FlatList` component is used to render the list of to-dos. Each item in the list has a "Remove" button to remove that specific task.

Real-World Example: Managing the State of a To-Do List in React Native

Let's walk through a complete example where we manage the state of a **to-do list** in a React Native app using Redux.

Step 1: Set Up Redux Store:

We've already covered setting up the Redux store, actions, and reducers in the previous section.

Step 2: Create the Todo App with Redux:

javascript

```
// App.js
```

```javascript
import React from 'react';
import { View, Text, Button } from 'react-native';
import TodoList from './TodoList';

function App() {
  return (
    <View style={{ flex: 1, justifyContent: 'center', alignItems: 'center' }}>
      <Text>React Native To-Do App with Redux</Text>
      <TodoList />
    </View>
  );
}

export default App;
```

- **App.js**: The main application component that renders the `TodoList` component.

Step 3: Complete Todo List Component:
javascript

```javascript
// TodoList.js
import React from 'react';
import { View, Text, Button, FlatList } from 'react-native';
```

```
import { useSelector, useDispatch } from 'react-
redux';
import { addTodo, removeTodo } from
'./actions/todoActions';

function TodoList() {
  const dispatch = useDispatch();
  const todos = useSelector((state) =>
state.todos);

  const handleAddTodo = () => {
    const newTodo = { id:
Math.random().toString(), text: 'New To-Do' };
    dispatch(addTodo(newTodo));
  };

  const handleRemoveTodo = (id) => {
    dispatch(removeTodo(id));
  };

  return (
    <View>
      <Button title="Add Todo"
onPress={handleAddTodo} />
      <FlatList
        data={todos}
        keyExtractor={(item) => item.id}
        renderItem={({ item }) => (
          <View>
```

```
        <Text>{item.text}</Text>
        <Button  title="Remove"  onPress={()
=> handleRemoveTodo(item.id)} />
      </View>
    )}
  />
  </View>
);
}
```

```
export default TodoList;
```

Step 4: Testing the App

To test the app:

1. Run `npm start` to open the Expo project in your browser or mobile app.
2. The app should display a button to add new to-dos and a list of existing tasks. You can add tasks and remove them using the buttons.

Conclusion

In this chapter, we explored how to manage **mobile state** in React Native applications using **Redux**:

- We learned about the core concepts of **Redux**, including **actions**, **reducers**, and the **store**.

- We set up Redux in a React Native app and created actions to **add** and **remove** tasks from a to-do list.

- We built a **simple to-do app** in React Native that uses Redux to manage the state of tasks, allowing users to add and remove to-dos.

Redux is a powerful tool for managing complex state in React Native applications, and it can significantly improve your app's scalability and maintainability. In the next chapter, we will dive into **navigation in React Native** using **React Navigation**, one of the most widely used libraries for managing navigation in mobile apps.

CHAPTER 25

BUILDING PROGRESSIVE WEB APPS (PWAS) WITH REACT

Introduction to Progressive Web Apps and Their Benefits

A **Progressive Web App (PWA)** is a type of application that uses modern web technologies to deliver a native-like experience to users while still being accessible via a browser. PWAs aim to combine the best of both web and mobile applications by offering features like offline support, push notifications, and fast loading times, all while being accessible via a simple URL.

Key Features of PWAs:

1. **Offline Capabilities**:
   o   PWAs use **service workers** to enable offline functionality by caching assets and data, allowing the app to work even without an internet connection.

2. **Responsive Design**:
   o   PWAs are designed to be responsive and provide a seamless user experience on desktops, tablets, and mobile devices.

3. **App-Like Experience**:

   o PWAs offer an app-like experience with smooth transitions, easy navigation, and quick loading times, similar to native mobile applications.

4. **Push Notifications**:

   o PWAs can send push notifications, which can engage users even when the app is not open.

5. **Easy Installation**:

   o PWAs can be installed directly from the browser onto the user's device home screen without requiring an app store. This is done by simply adding the app to the home screen from the browser.

6. **Improved Performance**:

   o PWAs load quickly and have fast response times, even on slow networks, thanks to caching, lazy loading, and other performance optimizations.

Why Use PWAs?

- **Cost-Effective**: Building a single PWA for multiple platforms (iOS, Android, web) is more cost-effective than building separate native apps.

- **No App Store Restrictions**: PWAs can be deployed and updated directly from the web, avoiding the limitations and approval processes of app stores.

- **Offline Functionality**: PWAs provide valuable offline functionality, which is crucial for users in areas with limited or unreliable internet access.

Setting Up a PWA with React

To turn a React application into a Progressive Web App, we need to make a few modifications. React provides a simple way to enable PWA functionality through the `create-react-app` tool, which comes with built-in support for service workers and other PWA features.

Step 1: Create a React App

If you haven't already created a React app, you can use `create-react-app` to generate a new project that supports PWA out of the box.

bash

```
npx create-react-app my-pwa-app
cd my-pwa-app
```

Step 2: Enable PWA Support in React

`create-react-app` comes with PWA support by default, but it requires you to make a few changes to enable it.

1. **Service Worker**: In `src/index.js`, you'll find a service worker registration that is disabled by default:

```javascript
javascript
```

```javascript
// Change this:
serviceWorker.unregister();

// To this:
serviceWorker.register();
```

The `serviceWorker.register()` call is what makes your app a PWA by enabling the service worker. The service worker allows your app to cache resources and function offline.

2. **Manifest File**: In the `public` folder, there is a `manifest.json` file that defines how the app should behave when installed on the user's device. Make sure to modify this file to suit your needs:

```json
json
```

```json
{
  "short_name": "PWA App",
  "name": "React Progressive Web App",
  "icons": [
    {
      "src": "favicon.ico",
      "sizes": "64x64 32x32 24x24 16x16",
```

```json
      "type": "image/x-icon"
    },
    {
      "src": "android-chrome-192x192.png",
      "sizes": "192x192",
      "type": "image/png"
    },
    {
      "src": "android-chrome-512x512.png",
      "sizes": "512x512",
      "type": "image/png"
    }
  ],
  "start_url": ".",
  "display": "standalone",
  "background_color": "#ffffff",
  "theme_color": "#000000"
}
```

- **short_name**: A short name for the app that will appear on the user's home screen.
- **name**: The full name of the app.
- **icons**: Icons that represent the app in different sizes.
- **start_url**: The URL that the app should open to when launched.
- **display**: Defines how the app should be displayed on the user's device. standalone makes the app look like a native app without the browser chrome (URL bar, etc.).

- **`background_color`** and **`theme_color`**: Control the background and theme colors used in the app when launched from the home screen.

3. **Testing the PWA**:
   - Run the app locally using:

   ```bash
   bash
   ```

   ```bash
   npm start
   ```

   - Visit the app in your browser and open **DevTools**. Under the **Application** tab, you can check if the service worker is registered and if the manifest is configured correctly.

Real-World Example: Converting a React App into a PWA

Let's take an existing **To-Do App** and convert it into a PWA with offline capabilities, app-like experience, and push notifications.

Step 1: Convert the To-Do App into a PWA

1. **Install `create-react-app` (if not already done)**:

```bash
bash
```

```bash
npx create-react-app todo-pwa
```

```
cd todo-pwa
```

2. **Modify the App**: Edit the `src/App.js` to add basic To-Do functionality (adding tasks, removing tasks, etc.):

```javascript
import React, { useState } from 'react';

function App() {
  const [task, setTask] = useState('');
  const [tasks, setTasks] = useState([]);

  const addTask = () => {
    if (task) {
      setTasks([...tasks,          {          id:
Math.random().toString(), text: task }]);
      setTask('');
    }
  };

  const removeTask = (id) => {
    setTasks(tasks.filter((task) => task.id !==
id));
  };

  return (
    <div style={{ padding: '20px' }}>
      <h1>To-Do App</h1>
      <input
```

```
        type="text"
        placeholder="Add a new task"
        value={task}
        onChange={(e)                        =>
setTask(e.target.value)}
        style={{ padding: '10px', marginRight:
'10px' }}
      />
      <button             onClick={addTask}>Add
Task</button>
      <ul style={{ marginTop: '20px' }}>
        {tasks.map((task) => (
          <li key={task.id}>
            {task.text}
            <button       onClick={()           =>
removeTask(task.id)} style={{ marginLeft: '10px'
}}>
              Remove
            </button>
          </li>
        ))}
      </ul>
    </div>
  );
}

export default App;
```

Step 2: Enable Service Worker for Offline Support

1. **Enable Service Worker**: In `src/index.js`, change `serviceWorker.unregister()` to `serviceWorker.register()`:

javascript

```
import React from 'react';
import ReactDOM from 'react-dom';
import './index.css';
import App from './App';
import * as serviceWorker from './serviceWorker';

ReactDOM.render(<App />,
document.getElementById('root'));

// Register service worker for offline support
serviceWorker.register();
```

Step 3: Update the Manifest File

1. In the `public/manifest.json`, update the app's name, icon, and other properties as discussed earlier:

json

```
{
  "short_name": "ToDo App",
  "name": "Progressive To-Do App",
```

```json
"icons": [
  {
    "src": "favicon.ico",
    "sizes": "64x64 32x32 24x24 16x16",
    "type": "image/x-icon"
  },
  {
    "src": "android-chrome-192x192.png",
    "sizes": "192x192",
    "type": "image/png"
  },
  {
    "src": "android-chrome-512x512.png",
    "sizes": "512x512",
    "type": "image/png"
  }
],
"start_url": ".",
"display": "standalone",
"background_color": "#ffffff",
"theme_color": "#000000"
}
```

Step 4: Build the App for Production

1. **Build the PWA**:

bash

```bash
npm run build
```

2. **Test the PWA**:

  o Open the `build` folder and deploy the app using a local server (you can use services like surge.sh or Netlify).

  o Test the app by opening it in a browser and adding it to your home screen. It should now function like a native app with offline support.

Conclusion

In this chapter, we learned how to build **Progressive Web Apps (PWAs)** with React. We:

- Discussed the **benefits of PWAs**, including offline capabilities, fast loading times, and improved SEO.
- Set up a **PWA in React** by enabling service workers, configuring a manifest file, and using caching strategies for offline support.
- Converted a basic **To-Do app** into a PWA, demonstrating the power of React for building mobile-friendly, app-like experiences.

PWAs provide a way to deliver a fast, reliable, and engaging user experience, and they are a great choice for building cross-platform web applications. In the next chapter, we will explore **advanced**

mobile app development with **React Native**, focusing on performance optimization and platform-specific features.

CHAPTER 26

DEPLOYING REACT APPS

Overview of Deployment Strategies for React Apps

Once you've developed your **React app**, the next step is to deploy it and make it accessible to users. There are several deployment strategies available depending on your app's complexity and requirements. Whether you're building a **static site**, a **dynamic app**, or a **Progressive Web App (PWA)**, deploying React apps is relatively straightforward with the right tools and platforms.

Common Deployment Strategies:

1. **Static Hosting**:
   - If your React app is a single-page application (SPA) or a static site, you can deploy it to a **static hosting platform**. These platforms are optimized for serving static files like HTML, CSS, JavaScript, and images.
   - **Popular platforms**: Netlify, Vercel, GitHub Pages.

2. **Backend-Integrated Hosting**:
   - If your React app requires a server to handle backend logic (e.g., APIs, databases), you can

deploy it to a platform that supports both the front-end and back-end.

- o **Popular platforms**: Heroku, AWS, DigitalOcean.

3. **Containerized Deployment**:
   - o For more complex applications, you can package your React app and back-end into Docker containers and deploy them to container orchestration platforms.
   - o **Popular platforms**: Docker, Kubernetes, AWS ECS.

In this chapter, we'll focus on deploying a React app to popular platforms like **Netlify**, **Vercel**, and **Heroku**—all of which make deployment easy and fast, especially for developers who prefer simple solutions for web apps.

Deploying to Popular Platforms

1. Deploying to Netlify

Netlify is one of the most popular platforms for deploying React apps, offering seamless integration with Git repositories and automatic deployments whenever changes are pushed. It is an excellent choice for **static sites**, including **PWAs**.

Steps to Deploy React App to Netlify:

1. **Create a React App**: If you don't already have a React app, create one using `create-react-app`:

bash

```
npx create-react-app my-react-app
cd my-react-app
```

2. **Build the React App**: Build the app for production using the following command:

bash

```
npm run build
```

This creates a `build` folder containing the optimized files that you'll deploy.

3. **Create a Netlify Account**:
   o   Go to Netlify and sign up for a free account if you don't have one.
   o   You can use GitHub, GitLab, or Bitbucket to sign in.

4. **Deploy via the Netlify UI**:
   o   On the Netlify dashboard, click on **"New site from Git"**.

- Choose your Git repository (GitHub, GitLab, Bitbucket), and authorize Netlify to access your repository.
- Select the repository containing your React app.
- For build settings, Netlify will automatically detect that you're using **React** and set the build command to `npm run build` and the publish directory to `/build`.

5. **Deploy the Site**:
   - After configuring the build settings, click on **Deploy site**.
   - Netlify will build and deploy your app automatically.
   - Once the deployment is complete, Netlify will provide a public URL for your app.

6. **Custom Domain (Optional)**:
   - You can set a custom domain if you have one, or use the default Netlify subdomain.
   - To add a custom domain, go to the "Domain settings" on the Netlify dashboard and follow the instructions.

2. Deploying to Vercel

Vercel is another great platform for deploying React apps, known for its simplicity and performance. It's especially well-suited for static sites, serverless functions, and PWAs.

Steps to Deploy React App to Vercel:

1. **Create a React App**: If you don't already have a React app, create one using `create-react-app`:

   bash

   ```
   npx create-react-app my-vercel-app
   cd my-vercel-app
   ```

2. **Build the React App**: Build the app for production:

   bash

   ```
   npm run build
   ```

3. **Create a Vercel Account**:
   - Go to Vercel and sign up with GitHub, GitLab, or Bitbucket.

4. **Deploy via GitHub Integration**:
   - Once signed in, click on **"New Project"**.
   - Import your project from your Git repository.
   - Select the React app repository.

- o Vercel will automatically detect the React framework and set up the build command and output directory.

5. **Deploy the Site**:
   - o Click on **Deploy**.
   - o Vercel will build and deploy the app, and you'll receive a **public URL**.

6. **Custom Domain (Optional)**:
   - o You can set up a custom domain by going to the "Domains" section in the Vercel dashboard and following the setup instructions.

---

3. Deploying to Heroku

Heroku is a cloud platform that supports both front-end and back-end applications. It is a great option for deploying full-stack apps, but it can also be used to deploy static sites like React apps.

Steps to Deploy React App to Heroku:

1. **Create a React App**: If you don't have a React app, create one using `create-react-app`:

bash

```
npx create-react-app my-heroku-app
cd my-heroku-app
```

2. **Build the React App**: Build the app for production:

```bash
```

```bash
npm run build
```

3. **Create a Heroku Account**:
   o Go to Heroku and sign up for an account if you don't have one.

4. **Install the Heroku CLI**:
   o Download and install the Heroku CLI from Heroku's website.

5. **Deploy to Heroku**:
   o Initialize a Git repository in your project folder (if you haven't already):

```bash
```

```bash
git init
```

   o Create a `Procfile` in the root of your project to tell Heroku how to run the app:

```makefile
```

```makefile
web: serve -s build
```

This command tells Heroku to serve the static files from the `build` directory.

o   Install **serve** globally to serve the app:

```bash
```

```bash
npm install -g serve
```

6. **Commit the Changes**:

```bash
```

```bash
git add .
git commit -m "Prepare app for Heroku deployment"
```

7. **Login to Heroku**:

Run the following command to log in to Heroku through the terminal:

```bash
```

```bash
heroku login
```

8. **Create a Heroku App**:

Create a new app on Heroku:

```bash
```

```bash
heroku create
```

9. **Deploy the App**:

Push the code to Heroku:

bash

```
git push heroku master
```

After the app is deployed, you will get a **public URL** for your app.

Real-World Example: Deploying a React App to Netlify

Let's go through the steps to deploy a simple **React app** to **Netlify**.

Step 1: Build the App

First, build the React app using the following command:

bash

```
npm run build
```

This will generate a `build` folder containing the optimized files ready for deployment.

Step 2: Sign Up for Netlify

1. Go to Netlify and sign up or log in with your GitHub account.
2. On the **dashboard**, click **New site from Git**.

Step 3: Connect GitHub Repository

1. Netlify will ask you to link your GitHub repository. Choose the repository that contains your React app.
2. Select the **branch** you want to deploy (usually main or master).
3. Netlify will automatically detect that you are using **React** and will set the build command to npm run build and the publish directory to /build.

Step 4: Deploy the App

Click **Deploy Site**, and Netlify will build and deploy your app.

After deployment, Netlify will provide a public URL (like https://react-app-12345.netlify.app) where your app can be accessed.

Step 5: (Optional) Add a Custom Domain

You can add a custom domain through Netlify's interface under the **Domain Settings** section.

Conclusion

In this chapter, we explored different deployment strategies for React apps and learned how to deploy them to popular platforms such as **Netlify**, **Vercel**, and **Heroku**:

- We discussed the benefits of **Netlify** and **Vercel** for deploying static React apps with automatic builds from GitHub.
- We also covered deploying React apps to **Heroku**, which is better suited for full-stack applications that require server-side logic.
- We walked through a **real-world example** of deploying a React app to Netlify, providing a step-by-step guide for beginners.

React app deployment is now easier than ever, thanks to platforms like **Netlify** and **Vercel**. In the next chapter, we will explore **continuous integration and continuous deployment (CI/CD)** with services like **GitHub Actions** to automate the deployment process.

CHAPTER 27

KEEPING UP WITH REACT: ADVANCED CONCEPTS AND RESOURCES

Exploring the Latest React Features and Trends

React is a powerful and constantly evolving library, with new features and updates being introduced frequently. Staying up-to-date with these changes is crucial for React developers who want to leverage the latest advancements and best practices in web and mobile development.

1. Concurrent Rendering (React 18 and beyond)

One of the most significant changes in recent React versions is the introduction of **Concurrent Rendering**. This feature allows React to interrupt rendering work to work on other tasks, providing a smoother user experience, particularly in complex or interactive apps.

Key Benefits:

- **Improved responsiveness**: React can prioritize important updates (like user interactions) over less critical ones (like background tasks).

- **Suspense for data fetching**: React Suspense, in conjunction with concurrent rendering, allows you to declaratively wait for data before rendering components. This makes data fetching more efficient and reduces the amount of loading states in the UI.

To enable concurrent rendering, you must opt-in using the createRoot API in React 18:

```javascript
import ReactDOM from 'react-dom/client';

const root =
ReactDOM.createRoot(document.getElementById('ro
ot'));
root.render(<App />);
```

2. React Server Components (Experimental)

React Server Components are a new experimental feature that allows you to render components on the server without sending the JavaScript code to the client. This can improve the performance of large React apps by reducing the JavaScript bundle size and offloading rendering to the server.

308

- **Server-Side Rendering (SSR)** and **static site generation (SSG)** are already widely used, but React Server Components aim to take this a step further by optimizing component-level rendering on the server.

This feature is still experimental and not fully integrated into React, but it's worth keeping an eye on as it evolves.

3. Suspense for Data Fetching

React's **Suspense** is an important feature for handling asynchronous operations like data fetching and code splitting. With **Suspense for data fetching**, you can declaratively specify loading states when fetching data for your components.

Example of using Suspense:

javascript

```javascript
const UserProfile = React.lazy(() =>
import('./UserProfile'));

function App() {
  return (
    <Suspense fallback={<div>Loading...</div>}>
      <UserProfile />
    </Suspense>
  );
}
```

This feature is being enhanced further, and with React 18, the **Suspense** API is becoming more powerful, allowing it to handle data fetching in a declarative way, reducing the need for manual loading indicators.

4. React Hooks: Advancements and New Patterns

React hooks continue to evolve, with new hooks introduced to make state and side-effect management more flexible and powerful. Some notable hooks include:

- **useId**: Introduced to provide unique IDs across the server and client for SSR compatibility.
- **useSyncExternalStore**: For subscribing to external stores in a way that's compatible with concurrent rendering.
- **useDeferredValue**: Helps to defer non-urgent updates, improving responsiveness during complex updates or rendering tasks.

These hooks allow developers to create more flexible, maintainable, and performance-optimized React apps.

How to Keep Learning and Evolving as a React Developer

The React ecosystem evolves quickly, and it's important to continue learning to stay competitive and keep up with new trends

310

and best practices. Here are some effective ways to continue growing as a React developer:

1. Follow Official React Resources

- **React Blog**: The official React blog is a great resource for staying up to date with new features, releases, and breaking changes. The React team frequently posts detailed explanations of new updates and best practices.
- **React Documentation**: The official React documentation is always the best place to start when learning new features or reviewing core concepts.

2. Participate in Open-Source Projects

- Contributing to open-source projects on GitHub is an excellent way to learn more advanced React concepts and interact with other developers. You can explore **React libraries**, help improve existing projects, and learn from real-world codebases.

3. Engage with the React Community

- **Stack Overflow** and **Reddit (r/reactjs)** are valuable places to ask questions, share knowledge, and engage with other React developers.
- Attend React conferences like **React Conf** and participate in **local meetups** to stay connected with industry trends.

4. Work on Real Projects

- The best way to deepen your understanding of React is by building real-world projects. Whether it's a personal project, a freelance job, or a side project for practice, working on something that interests you will expose you to various challenges and help you learn advanced techniques.

5. Explore Related Libraries and Tools

React has a large ecosystem of libraries and tools that complement it and enhance its capabilities. Here are a few to explore:

- **React Router**: For handling navigation and routing in React applications.
- **Redux** and **React Query**: For managing state, side effects, and data fetching in complex apps.
- **React Native**: For building mobile applications using the same React concepts.
- **Next.js**: A powerful React framework that offers server-side rendering, static site generation, and other advanced features.

Resources for Advanced React Topics and Full-Stack Development

To continue your learning journey and master **advanced React** topics and full-stack development, here are some valuable resources:

1. Advanced React Courses and Books

- **"Fullstack Open"**: A free course that covers advanced React concepts and full-stack development with React, Node.js, GraphQL, and MongoDB. Available at Fullstack Open.

- **"React - Up and Running" by Stoyan Stefanov**: This book dives deep into React concepts and is perfect for developers who want to go beyond the basics.

- **"The Road to React" by Robin Wieruch**: A practical guide that covers advanced React features, including React hooks, React Router, and context API, and guides you through building full-stack apps with React.

2. Full-Stack Development with React

Full-stack development with React is about combining React on the front-end with technologies like Node.js, Express, and MongoDB (or SQL) on the back-end. A few resources to master full-stack React development:

- **"Learning Full-Stack JavaScript Development"** by Eric Bush: This book covers full-stack development using React, Express, and MongoDB.
- **"The Complete Guide to Full Stack JavaScript"** by Maximilian Schwarzmüller on Udemy: A complete course covering React, Node.js, and databases.

3. Community and Tutorials

- **Dev.to**: A fantastic platform where React developers share blog posts, tutorials, and insights. Follow tags like #react, #reactnative, and #javascript to stay updated.
- **Egghead.io**: Egghead offers high-quality short tutorials on advanced React topics, including hooks, state management, and testing.
- **Frontend Masters**: Offers courses for React, Redux, and full-stack development, taught by industry professionals.

Final Thoughts on Mastering React and Building Dynamic Web and Mobile Apps

React is an incredibly powerful library for building dynamic, interactive user interfaces, whether for web or mobile apps. As a React developer, it's important to:

- Stay current with new features and updates, like **Concurrent Rendering**, **React Server Components**, and **Suspense for Data Fetching**.
- Master state management techniques with **Redux** and **React Query**.
- Build real-world projects to apply your knowledge and tackle real-world problems.
- Explore the wider ecosystem, including tools like **Next.js**, **React Native**, and **GraphQL**, to build full-stack applications and mobile apps.

By continuing to build and learn from the React community, you'll become a proficient React developer, capable of building powerful, scalable web and mobile applications. The journey of learning React never truly ends, as new updates and best practices continue to emerge.

Keep coding, stay curious, and always be open to new ideas and technologies. You are now equipped with the skills to build the future of the web and mobile apps with React.